Creativity to Reinvent Your Life

Reflections on Change, Intuition and Spiritual Alchemy

Creativity to Reinvent Your Life

Reflections on Change, Intuition and
Spiritual Alchemy

Miriam Subirana Vilanova

BOOKS

Winchester, UK
Washington, USA

First published by O-Books, 2010
O Books is an imprint of John Hunt Publishing Ltd., The Bothy, Deershot Lodge, Park Lane, Ropley,
Hants, SO24 0BE, UK
office1@o-books.net
www.o-books.com

For distributor details and how to order please visit the 'Ordering' section on our website.

Text copyright: Miriam Subirana Vilanova 2009

ISBN: 978 1 84694 361 4

A CIP catalogue record for this book is available from the British Library.

Design: Stuart Davies

Original Title: Creatividad para reinventar tu vida. Reflexiones sobre el cambio, la intuición y la
alquimia espiritual. RBA-Integral. Translation from original in Spanish by Caroline Wilson

Cover Illustration: Embrace Life II, painting by Miriam Subirana

Printed in the UK by CPI Antony Rowe
Printed in the USA by Offset Paperback Mfrs, Inc

We operate a distinctive and ethical publishing philosophy in all
areas of our business, from our global network of authors to
production and worldwide distribution.

CONTENTS

I dedicate this book
To all those who dare to transform their life creatively and thus
collaborate in creating a new world.
To those who, with their creativity, bring the energy of silence
to the world.
To those who go into the magnificence of their being and shine
with all their strengths. They illuminate as they pass and
inspire others to shine.

When we really love ourselves and each other, everything flows in our life.

Prologue

Every act of creation drinks from the fountain of life. Those who connect to that fountain become creative beings. Because of this the author of this book is profuse when it comes to creating. There are fast authors and others who are slow, as there are fast artists and slow artists, but this has nothing to do with the quality of a book or a work of art, but rather with the capacity one has to connect to the origin of that creativity that passes through one, which is life itself. So that the profusion of books — and also of paintings — of Miriam Subirana is an indication of her closeness to the springs that run through her. The book invites us to this: to drink from the stream of life that flows permanently everywhere, inside and outside of us.

Those who know the previous books of Miriam Subirana will recognize her style straight away: agile sentences that flow, ideas that connect to each other with a great liveliness, as if the idea precedes the word that runs straggling behind her so as not to let it get away. But we do not have to fear, because nothing gets away, rather everything returns again and again in different ways, from diverse angles, to always encourage the same, from different perspectives: the delight of being co-creators of an existence which is given to us so that we might expand it.

One of the most thought-provoking aspects of this piece of work is that not only does it describe the goal, but it examines in tiny detail the processes and the itinerary to reach it. If in her previous books the processes of how to reach that freedom of living were described, in the present book she speaks at length of the processes of creativity. She details the spaces that make it possible, as well as the blockages that prevent it. And it would be an error to laud only its easiness. It is also necessary to describe the struggle and the agony, because, without them, there is not growth but rather an indolent repetition of the same. To create and co-create means to die, to release the old, to have the courage to free oneself of habits and layers in which, protected, we keep ourselves busy and we stupefy ourselves. This letting go is not arbitrary, because we also have to know how to stay with what sustains us. In order to create, one has to choose, and to choose means to renounce. But the renunciation does not take away, renunciation gives. It gives on another plane than the previous one. When liberation takes place we enter into a new perception of reality, because we do not pick up on things as they are, rather as we are.

The origin of creativity, which here is synonymous with life, has diverse planes and the last of all of them is the one that religious traditions identify with God. But this is a word that has to be used with care, since it has been abused. Our culture is doing without the word God. In these pages it appears under multiple names, both from the East and the West, so that nobody feels excluded and to avoid it causing rejection. It appears with the different names that the mystics of the diverse traditions have given it and that psychologists identify with the archetypes.

In sum, we have before us an invitation to unfold all the potential of creative freedom that we have, and it helps us to understand that what is at stake is much more than doing things; it is to turn one's own existence into a creative act. To do so we have been brought into existence: to give an unrepeatable form to the portion of Life that has been placed in our hands. Being depositaries of the co-creating act of existence like this is permanently made up of two tempos: receiving and giving, taking on and turning one's own life into an offering.

Those who live thus, form a part of Something much greater than themselves and they discover it flowing everywhere, like in the pages of this book.

Javier Melloni

Introduction

This book is for you and about you.

It will help you to awaken, discover and use your immense creative potential in order to live better here and now. You will discover dimensions of creativity that will allow you to connect to your deepest feeling, so that all your energy can emerge in the best way possible.

Getting out of our routine, improving a relationship, or reinventing oneself are some of the many benefits that the fact of being creative brings to us.

You are creative

In this book I am not going to write about the artistic creative expression of professional artists who are experienced, recognized and expert. **I am going to look at creativity as a gift that each one of us has.** We are going to look at the different ways of using our creativity for change.

The change

- From pain to wellbeing.
- From separation to union.
- From loneliness to creative solitude.
- From being trapped in a relationship to being free in it.
- From sadness to happiness.
- From submission to liberation.
- From repression to expression.
- From a closed heart to an open heart.
- From emotional defensiveness to emotional openness.
- From crying to joy.

You are capable of creating from different creative spaces. You can create beauty and friendship. You can sow happiness and cheerfulness. You can create reconciliation and peace. You can establish harmony and happiness. You can also create ill feeling and hate. You can generate rejection and abandonment. You can create a jungle or a garden. You can generate thorns or flowers. You can be fragrant or odorous. You can give out and love generously or beg for affection and attention.

You can. You can do so much and so well... You can be and shine. You can forgive and become free.

This book offers you the guidelines to having creative power in your hands. That way you will no longer be a shipwreck at the mercy of the currents, the waves and the wind; rather, you will be at the helm of your life.

The currents are the situations that you have lived through and that have left marks on you in the form of scars, of relationships that have to be ended, of aspects that you have to reconcile in yourself, of habits that control you. They are the underground currents that move within you and cause you worry, unease and anxiety.

The waves are the multiple influences that put pressure on you. Influences of people, situations, jobs, etc.

The winds are the cultural, religious and social conditionings, the economic, political and work conditionings, the sports team following conditionings... These winds come into our inner house and condition our decisions and actions.

If we do not hold on firmly to the helm of our life, the currents, the waves and the winds will continue to dominate us.

This book will offer you guidelines to discovering what it means for you to be at the helm, how to grasp it strongly and allow it to guide your life, as well as helping you to listen to your intuition, your inner teacher that stimulates true creativity.

In the next chapters you will find four words that can be interpreted in many ways. I want to be clear about how I understand and use them in this book. These terms are:

- Power.
- The ego.
- The soul.
- God.

Power

Power is a drug. It is difficult to become unused to it. "Influencing others' lives relieves us of our own doubts," Erich Fromm said. When people feel obliged to pay you attention, you have the option of rewarding or penalizing them. Power has a positive effect on our own insecurities.

Power is associated with control. The obsession to control is usually based on mistrust, the lack of real self-esteem, insecurity and the fear of uncertainty and freedom. Taken to its extreme it means an aversion to risk, resistance to change and the inhibition of one's own and others' creativity. The obsession for control often arises out of the incapacity to recognize and appreciate the value of spontaneity and happiness.

These factors related to the word power generate rejection, especially in 'spiritual' and personal development contexts.

When you read the word *power* in the pages to come, I will not be writing of that dimension of power but rather of the power that you have to rule in your life. Of the power of your consciousness to create or destroy, submit or be submitted. Of the power that you have to discern and decide. Of the power that makes you free. Of your personal power: of your energy, capacity, will and inner strength.

The ego and the soul

We have a multiple identity or multiple identities. Some have to do with our body:

- gender,
- age, and

- shape, height, beauty, color, etc.

Others have to do with our talents and capacities, with our role, our education, culture, profession.

And there are others, such as social class, the clan we belong to, etc.

There is also the identity connected to our religious or agnostic, political or cultural beliefs, on what is good or bad, what is wrong and what is right, what failure is and what success is, about life and the world in general.

Our identity is also our being, with its qualities and inner faculties. The same way that the body has organs, the consciousness also has 'organs', which are the mind, the intellect, the heart of being, of the soul (not the physical heart that pumps blood) and the memory: the store cupboards where we keep our memories, habits, tendencies and conditionings. In the center, at the heart of our being, is the voice of the consciousness. To reach it we have our intuition.

The soul is the conscious energy that lives in your body, it is you.

The ego is comprised of all the identities that identify the self and are *not* the self. It would be like the layers of an onion. The ego covers over the self. As I explained in the book *Live in Freedom*, the essential qualities of the self, the soul, are like the five points of a star: peace, love, purity, innate wisdom and freedom.

The ego, understood as a limited identity of the bodily self, makes us think and feel that objects, people, lands and many other things 'are ours'. From the feeling of possession come, among others:

- attachment,
- greed,
- controlling,

- fear (of losing what you consider yours),
- sadness (when you lose what you considered yours) and
- anger (for having lost it).

When you read the word ego in the pages to come, I am referring to the external layers of your identity which are temporal, acquired and not innate.

When I talk about the *being*, the *consciousness* or the *soul*, I am referring to you: you, the being of conscious energy that in the beginning was innocent, clean, free, loving and peaceful.

God

God is the creator and, we, His creation.

Others say that God is our creation. He is our autosuggestion and our invention. We need a God and so we have invented one.

For me, it is clear that three kinds of energy exist:

- The energy of matter: it is neither created nor destroyed; it is transformed. It goes from the essence to expansion and from expansion to the essence. From order to chaos, to entropy, and from entropy, to order.
- The energy of human consciousness, the energy of the soul: it is neither created nor destroyed; it is transformed. It goes from the essence to expansion and from expansion to the essence. From order to chaos, to entropy, and from entropy, to order.
- The divine energy, the energy of God: it is neither created nor destroyed. It is. Eternally, it is. It is the energy of the origin, stable, pure; it has never been polluted nor entered into entropy.

When I, in the consciousness of the soul, am aligned with the energy of my body, which is material created from the four elements — water, earth, fire and air — and I am aligned with

God, the order of my being is restored.

In a closed system, the elements go from order to chaos, to entropy. Only an external energy is able to return order to entropy. For example, a used battery: it is connected to a source of external supply in order to recover its energy. It cannot recharge itself.

When I, the soul, reconnect with God, I recover my original energy. My eyes, the windows of the soul, shine. Have you seen the shine in the eyes of a child? Ekhart Tolle expresses it beautifully for us when he talks to us about babies, telling us that they are fragile, delicate, not yet established in the material. Through them an innocence shines, a sweetness and beauty that are not of this world. He is speaking to us of the energy of the soul.

In that connection with the divine, my mind creates elevated thoughts. My heart creates pure feelings. My body is the temple of the soul, and each one of its cells vibrates with positivity.

If **you do not believe in God**, this book will act as a bridge for you towards the opening of your creativity and all your inner potential.

Open yourself to experimentation, to discovering the unknown, to remembering what you have forgotten, to unveiling the veil that covers the marvelous being that YOU are.

In the book I offer brief comments about some subjects. If I had gone deeper into everything, this book would have had six hundred pages, or more. I mention them because they are related to the purpose of the book. They can stimulate you to continue going deeper and discovering.

At the beginning of each chapter there is a summary of the map and direction that I go in that chapter. That way you will discover them as you read.

In the bibliographical references that I include at the end you will find the details of the authors and the books I mention in the quotes. For easier reading this information can be found at the end.

1

You Can Be More Creative

In this chapter I define briefly what creativity is. I offer you a broad vision of the characteristics of constructive and transformative creativity. I encourage you to discover it, practice it and live it in your life so that you can play a part in co-creating an eco-system that leaves the old paradigm of the ego-system behind.

Creativity is the capacity to create, invent, innovate, introduce, communicate, transmit, recreate, combine, associate, project, visualize, channel, express and transform. Creativity is a medium through which to transmit our motivations and intentions.

According to Osho, a guru from India, creativity is "the greatest rebellion in existence," and "the fragrance of individual freedom."

Creativity has many dimensions. Innovative creativity arises and comes out from within. **You can be more creative.**

In this book I am going to look at the creativity that is necessary in this time that we are living in: here and now. A creativity that allows us to **leave behind stressful routine**, the lack of union and non-connection with our essence. That **unites us** and leads us to find the necessary connections to help us as human beings to create a better reality for everyone.

A creativity that comes out of an **awakened consciousness** to create a new paradigm: a new world.

A creativity that doesn't only help you, but that accompanies you and brings others out of their bodily cages of selfish pleasure, of their mental prisons and their comfort zones. For this it has to be a **daring creativity**. To be **elevating and trans-**

forming. To transcend and lead others to transcend.

A creativity **that opens**. That opens our eyes **in order to see and become aware**. That opens closed hearts **to feel and be**. That opens limited minds to enter into the unlimited and into the sacred of existence. That opens, so that repressed beings might express their potential without fears.

A creativity that **is generous** and encourages us to go from a culture of clinging on to a culture of gratitude and generosity.

A creativity **that nourishes**. It is a creativity that unites and upholds. It neither destroys nor wounds. It sustains transformation so that people take the risk and do not return to their old patterns of behavior.

A creativity **in conjunction** with and associated to nature.

A creativity **that respects**. Out of respect we create with the energy of good feelings, of understanding and valuing the space of the other. It is a creativity that encourages and creates out of humility and not out of violent provocation.

A creativity that **offers space to be**, to exist and to allow the other to be.

A creativity that moves out of the energy of the awakened consciousness. That causes **another energy to circulate in the human system**, in the thoughts and feelings, in the mind, the intellect, the memory and the heart. An energy that opens windows: that awakens sleeping consciousnesses. It is an energy which facilitates positive transformation. It is healing and the creator of a new paradigm.

A **responsible and conscious creativity**. Each one of us is responsible for the experiences that we have. Let us be conscious that we create our own reality. Is this the reality that we want? Are we prepared to sacrifice ourselves in order to create a better reality for everyone? Not a painful and unhappy sacrifice, but rather a sacrifice of letting go of our ego and giving ourselves to the other.

A **constructive creativity**. In a world where it seems that we are creative through destroying, we should be capable of coming out of that inertia in order to build. Let's be clear:

- We destroy our body by feeding it bad thoughts, clinging to feelings of blame, victimism, hate and bitterness. Feeding it badly. Using it to oppress and damage.
- We destroy the harmony in our relationships because we are in the state of asking, needing and wanting the other to satisfy our needs and longing. When the other isn't as we would like them to be we destroy the harmony, generating a deep unhappiness.
- We destroy the environment, using the resources of nature without respect, for selfish, greedy and exploitative ends.

An **inclusive creativity that embraces,** welcomes and is generous generates a spirit of union, like the three musketeers: one for all and all for one. **Personal health, the health of the planet and the health of humanity depend on us all working creatively.** It is a generous creativity that empowers our collaborators and people close to us. It allows them to take decisions in the face of new or unforeseen situations that arise daily. It makes them able to manage the unexpected. And this makes us feel freer, more developed, more useful.

A creativity that **generates newness and makes a difference.** Beyond talent, craftsmanship and ability. It is necessary to use the vehicle of talent; the important thing is not to get lost in it, for it not to be an end in itself. The message and the messenger are what are essential. Let us go deeper into this aspect. Let us see what the intention underlying the talent is. Let us be clear and not lose ourselves in embellishing our image in order to appear something that we are not. Let us refine our talent and skills. Let us do it as best as we can. But don't let's disconnect from the essence.

A **practical creativity,** whose end is not to impress or give great ideas, but rather to generate a true transformation: a metamorphosis.

A **spiritual creativity**. We create from the spirit, with what we are. We create to go higher, touch the sublime and feel it.

An **individual but not selfish creativity**. What is the intention behind our creativity? Do we want to use creativity to carry on clinging? To keep power? Let us revise our intention and motivation so that our creativity is unique but not narcissistic, rather personal and universal.

With this creativity we will go from an **ego-system to an eco-system.** In the ego-system, everything is about me and mine: what can I get? What can I control? How can I have more power? In the ego-system we have lost trust. The ego-system lacks generosity, which means there is neither true leadership nor creativity. It does not allow for the emerging of the power of the knowledge, of the competences, of the talent and the motivation of each collaborator, because one is centered on oneself. If we don't allow this to arise, the innovation is not possible whereby there might be enthusiasm, collaboration and, above all, the risk of taking on new challenges. In the eco-system it is all about all of us. While we continue to have the ego-system as a culture, we will have serious problems that will put our survival into question and the culture of greed and violence will prevail.

Returning to the creative source

On unfolding all your sleeping creative potential an endless amount of possibilities appear before you and for you. You become a co-creator of a new culture in which the art of being and, from being, peace, love and beauty make up an intrinsic part of the same. For this, it is necessary to return to the essence, to the creative source of each human being, and, from there, to create a new being, and a new world.

This creative force of each human sometimes gets blocked and needs to be rediscovered. In the next chapters you will find many guidelines with which to reconnect to your creative source. We are going to rediscover our creative force. We will see what dimensions of creativity are necessary to live in this period of crisis, changes and uncertainties. We will also discover the dimensions of creativity necessary to create a new woman and man, and, in sum, to create a new world.

2

Personal Creativity

When we really love ourselves, everything flows in our life.

Personal creativity gives you strength; it pushes you and helps you to leave the cage that does not allow you to fly. It gives you the energy and inspiration that are necessary to reinvent yourself and renew yourself.

In this chapter we will see the basis of innovation and Einstein's formula for innovation. We will question what authentic newness is and how new what we consider to be new really is.

We will see how to use our external senses: hearing, eyes and lips, in order to listen, see and share from a different perspective that dares to go beyond the apparent. We will see how our inner faculties of thinking and feeling, the mind and the heart, can be renewed in order to think better and to feel in a healthier way.

In this chapter you will find the following subheadings:

Personal creativity

Reinventing oneself

Einstein's formula for innovation

How new is the new?

Life is to be felt, not thought

> *The hearing*
> *The eyes*
> *The lips*
> *The mind*
> *The heart*
> *The body*

Personal creativity

A personal creativity is necessary that challenges the self to advance towards new perspectives and new expressions, towards a greater altruism and generosity.

A creativity that **gives you the strength** to get out of being in the prison of a wrong dream. Sometimes, when we are young, we undertake a life project without knowing exactly what we are getting into, and later we realize that we are living out a mistaken dream: we don't want to be doing that job, nor be with that partner, nor in that place.

It is a creativity that **helps you** to see beyond the illusions and the apparent, to see the truth and to see yourself reflected in the mirror. It makes it possible for you to realize how others see you and how they respond to you. Do they trust you? Do you trust? It accompanies you in going through the veil, to un-veil, to un-cover and to trust again.

It is a creativity to **get out of routine**. Routine kills the soul; it is like a slow poison. In routine you lose motivation. What you were passionate about before is now routine, and you feel trapped by your own reality. Routine pulls you down, and when you consider a change, you quickly desist, since the routine consumes your energy.

It is a creativity that **pushes you**, getting you out of your comfort zones and your conformity. With it you transcend limits and overcome negative and limiting beliefs. The tragedy lies, according to the *Upanishads*, in the fear of losing the limitations. We need this push to overcome fear and to make the jump.

It is a creativity to **recreate and reinvent** the self. How does the new self emerge? Out of nothing? Let's look at the example of the tree: the old leaves fall, and they leave room for the new ones to be born. Each time the tender leaves are born they are something new, even though it is the same process: dying and being born. Each time they are new, those that are born. Therefore, we do not create from nothing. From the old the new is born.

It is a creativity that arises out of curiosity, observation and discovery. You learn to **be inspired** and you value beauty.

To connect to this innate creative force you should put down roots within you. That way you will come to **recognize** your magnificence and divinity and that of others. You connect to your inner Shakti, to your archetype, which I will write about in the next chapters.

We should stimulate the intellect in order to **understand**. Normally we look for external stimulus in order to get out of routine and that way we distract ourselves. But we continue asleep. To stimulate the intellect in such a way for it to understand we need to be introverted: to see within.

On seeing, you understand that your path in life is marked by a series of events. Among them are concrete episodes of relationships, jobs, births, deaths, changes of address, new interests, successes, failures, illnesses, accidents, achievements, openings, closures. The traumatic events also make up part of your path. Widening the context enough, you will be able to see how these events align and what their global meaning is in order to be more aware of your path in this life.

Out of this understanding there arises in you a creativity that allows you to use the power that you have to **interpret your experiences** in the way that you find the most favorable or the least limiting. We have the power to modify our beliefs and thus modify our way of seeing life. The result can be a new life and new physical conditions. The indirect consequence of that process, Eric Rolf tells us, is mental and physical health.

Reinventing oneself

We are living in a period of crisis. The ego-system is unsustainable and its creation is already beginning to collapse. This crisis invites us to reflect, to re-evaluate where we have put our priorities and to realize to what extent we consider ourselves responsible, as consumers, as producers and as citizens who belong to a privileged minority: one that has access to drinking water, that can read and write, that reads the newspaper, that lives under a roof, that has more than one meal a day.

This crisis is an invitation to innovate. We have to reinvent ourselves in order to survive and to take our families and, in general, civilization, forwards. The crisis offers us the opportunity and the responsibility to change consciously. NOW we should be effective. The NEW that we create has to be practical and sustainable.

The bases of **INNOVATION** are:

- necessity,
- clarity,
- enthusiasm,
- creativity, and
- taking risks.

Necessity. Unless we find ourselves pushed or even pressured to change, our clinging on to the known and our addictions to routine are such that we need a push in order to innovate. If not, we remain in the comfort of the known and of our habitual 'doses'. NOW change is not only necessary, it is vital. When we do not listen to or feel this necessity, it comes as imposed on us. Nature will impose it through a crisis, a collapse, a rupture, an accident, or an illness.

Clarity. Contrary to confusion. Out of confusion we move energy, but we stay stuck in the same place, or we even go backwards. We do not advance. Clarity allows us to decide, express and direct our energy in the right direction. Clarity happens when the future attraction of our dream, our purpose, is strong.

Enthusiasm makes what seems impossible possible. It moves transforming energy. (See the section 'A Vital Space of Enthusiasm', page 132.)

Creativity. Fundamental for true innovation.

Risk. Without risks there is no change. The base of risk is love and trust. Mother Teresa of Calcutta spoke thus to a group of top managers in an international management congress in San Francisco: "Do you want there to be change? Do you want your people to change? Do you know them? Do you love them? If you do not know your people deeply there will not be understanding between you, and without understanding there will not be trust. Do you love your people? Is there love in what you do? If there isn't love in you there will not be power or strength in your people. If there is no strength there is no passion. **Without strength or passion nobody will risk themselves. And without taking risks nothing will change.**"

To know your people you have to know yourself. To have a good relationship with others you have to have a good relationship with yourself.

There is nothing so big that the human being cannot overcome or solve it.

Einstein's formula for innovation

Einstein proposed a formula for innovation that I share here with you. It consists of four phases:

First: **understand** the situation, that is, what is really happening. See it from different perspectives. Look at it 'with a bird's eye view'; see all the landscape, not only a part. See out of openness and responsibility. Not out of blame. If we look for guilty parties, our vision will be totally subjective and the understanding will be unilateral. Let's understand the present reality created by an ego-system. Let's understand our responsibility.

Second: **discover** the right question. We live reality according to the questions we ask. The questions invite us to discover other aspects of reality that were ignored or unknown before. The questions lead us to suffer or to learn, to blame or to take responsibility, to awaken or to stay asleep.

Third: **create** images of possibility. Think from 'outside the box' of mental limitations. Dream. What can I offer? What would I most like to share?

Fourth: **develop** possible strategies. Practical creativity put into action.

Einstein showed that, if he had to resolve a problem in an hour and his life depended on it, he would devote 55 minutes to finding the right question and 5 minutes for the answer. **What is a right question? It is the question that does not reiterate the problem but rather transcends it.** For example, McDonald's, for some time the biggest company worldwide that takes on young people in their first job, had a problem in that many of these young people would leave the job in a short space of time. The managers asked themselves: What can we do so that our workers stay? This question identifies the problem and, therefore, it is not the right question, since it leaves us stuck in what doesn't work. A right question could be: how can we make people, when they leave, be better people? If we give them training, the result will be that they will stay longer with us. The result was the level of permanence of the new employees went from being a few months to a minimum of three years.

This formula of Einstein's invites us to develop the potential of our creativity: our vision, thought, possibilities, impartial observation, wide, and of a long reach. It leads us to detach ourselves from a 'stubborn' horizontal limited vision. To see a painting we cannot stick our noses onto it. We need to distance ourselves.

How new is the new?

Sometimes the innovation that we seek is only to keep us where we are: in emotional addiction, in keeping our privileges, properties, possessions, position and power. Therefore it is like a fake innovation as we stay where we are, which means it is neither reinventing ourselves nor innovating.

As I explained in the book *Live in Freedom*, one of the dependences that promotes the consumer society is novelty. We need to fill ourselves with new clothes, new products, new images, etc. Thus do we generate an addiction to novelty. It is an addiction of boredom, of inner emptiness. We get bored very quickly and we need something apparently new and different.

But – how new is the new? Sometimes the wrapping is new, the outside appearance. But it is still the same, with the same content. What kind of novelty and innovation are we looking for? If we want to innovate in order to carry on clinging on to comfort and selfish pleasures, we will not create a new world; rather we will keep ourselves in the old paradigm, in the ego-system.

That is, we will keep ourselves in:

- The old feelings, the known feelings, based on past experiences registered on our memory, which will determine our present choices.
- The old mind: clinging on and stuck to the body. A mind that thinks according to the body chemistry created by addictions to certain behaviors, feelings and past experiences.
- Greed: I want, I cling onto, I need to accumulate.
- Fear. Fear of loss, of solitude, of emptiness, and, as a Chinese proverb says: "He who is afraid of suffering, is already suffering fear." Out of fear, true creativity is blocked.
- Imposing our selfish needs to vanquish the other, to possess them, to 'be' more powerful.
- Repressing our true self, our highest longings.
- The culture of blame and reward.

We have created a culture of offering rewards so that you will make an effort to achieve them. If you don't achieve them, you feel guilty. The motivation of the action is the reward, not the quality of what you do. This culture has permeated religion, advertising and many other areas. False guarantees are given: if you do this, if you buy this, you will receive such and such a thing. If you follow such rules, you will receive the reward of heaven. If you follow seven steps to achieve success and prosperity you will achieve it, and if you don't follow them you will feel guilt or failure for not having followed them. If you don't follow certain commandments or rules you are afraid or you feel guilty.

The teaching and these promises are not necessarily wrong. It is true that each action carries a response with it, which can be a reward (or a punishment). The expression in the action may not be right when the motivation that leads us to the action is in the reward, not in the quality of the action, in the energy that you put into it, or in excellence, not even in an objective that transcends you and your limited self.

Life is for feeling, not for thinking

A personal creativity is transforming when it encourages the hearing, the eyes, the lips, minds, hearts and body to act and feel differently. It is a creativity that offers another perspective to see beyond the apparent, to see positively, to realize and understand.

THE HEARING

Go from hearing to listening. What you hear, what you listen to. How you listen. If you listen from the soul, the heart of being, you understand.

Knowing how to listen means seeing behind the word and listening to the heart, the intention and the need of the other.

Knowing how to listen is to be in harmony with people's needs, to be in harmony with nature and be in harmony with what the situation tells you. When you are in harmony, you touch, you open and you liberate. You are in harmony with something because it resonates in you. Something touches your inner being.

We don't communicate with each other well because there is too much noise in our mind, and in our imagination. We have so many interferences that we cannot listen nor be in harmony.

When inside you there are mixes (feelings, selfish interests, mental interferences), you only listen to what you want to. This leads to bad interpretation, to misunderstandings and a lack of communication. Your listening is neither impartial nor global. You judge.

You have to weigh up, measure and discern what you hear so as not to consume heaviness. Not to be like a rubbish bin that picks up everything it hears. Germs come from the rubbish, causing illnesses. If you listen to something erroneous you can let it go out of the other ear, but if you accumulate what you listen to and speculate, imagine and project, you end up ill.

There are aspects of our life that, at different moments, seek our attention. Normally that implies a certain level of crisis, because if there is not a crisis we do not usually listen to the deep messages that lead us to true transformation.

Life speaks to you, and, if you are attentive, you will understand the message; sooner or later it will reach you, it will touch your soul and it will open you to a new understanding of the meaning of what is happening in your life and of the steps that you have to take.

Let us sharpen our hearing so that life doesn't have to speak louder. So that we can listen to the signs and act in consequence.

THE EYES

A new way of looking arises out of a new perception. We create illusions and mirages basing ourselves on erroneous perceptions. Let us leave the old perception that arises out of false or temporal beliefs. Beliefs are like walking sticks that help us for a time to cross a difficult stretch of the road. Once we have crossed it, we should have the courage to let go of the stick. That belief, that walking stick, is no longer of use to us. It limits our vision of life and our capacity to act. Let's not be afraid of letting go. Let's trust.

A new way of looking arises out of focusing your vision on the unlimited, not on the limited. On the great painting of life and not on the little puddle that you are in. As the *Upanishads* tell us: "You don't have to remove the clouds to realize the space. Where your consciousness lies, you *see*. Either you see the phenomenon or you see the Reality." You decide.

We have eyes to see the physical and the world that surrounds us. Let us open the inner eye, the eye of wisdom, to understand how to get back happiness, love, harmony and complete peace in our lives. The invisible is what gives power and meaning to the visible.

THE LIPS

Words create realities and move energies. Creativity helps us to express ourselves and to know how to talk with gentleness and meaning. To talk the necessary amount.

The word is a medium. But let's remember that nothing of what is said is infallible. We should know how to go beyond the word. Let us be aware that the words do not always reflect the person. They can be a trap or a defense. Someone may speak with talent but their personal life is a 'disaster'.

Let's be aware of the power of words. When what you think, say and feel is the same, your words are charged with power. Your energy is aligned.

Words can harm. When we judge what the other says and jump rapidly to conclusions according to what the other says, we don't communicate with each other adequately. Our listening is partial and our words are not wise. They arise out of rapid judgments.

Saint Paul says: "You must let no unwholesome word come out of your mouth, but only what is beneficial for the building up of the one in need, that it may give grace to those who hear"

(Ephesians 4:29).

THE MIND

You have the power to use your mind as you want. 'You', the consciousness, you have the power to govern and control your mind and intellect.

As quantum physics has shown, each one of us is the creator of our physical reality. Our thoughts create the reality. What we think about ourselves turns into our truth and our experience. The thoughts that we think and the words that we speak create our experiences.

Thoughts often arise from beliefs. The beliefs create the reality to a point where to believe and create are the same.

Each thought that we think is creating our present and our future. Let's remain at a distance from the thoughts that create problems and pain.

When we create peace, harmony and balance in our mind, these values will settle into our lives.

We have to know how to observe thoughts, since the more we identify with what we think, the more we distance ourselves from our essence, from our spiritual dimension. The thoughts are limited and variable: now you think one thing and the next minute another.

Being alert and knowing how to use the mind well is essential for a true transformation. One thing is what you think you believe and another is what in reality you experience. If you get lost in your mind, in thought, you disconnect from your essence. It is good to be aware of what you are thinking. Try for the thought not to be an escape. When the thought is automatic, it is not a conscious creation. **Without being conscious, you cannot transform**.

THE HEART

Your feelings create your experiences. With feelings you attract towards you or you distance from yourself situations and people. When you change your feelings, all the rest will change. Replace negative feelings, unwanted feelings, with other positive, constructive feelings, transforming and healing.

Don't repress or oppress, or allow others to do so to you. If they do it to you, it is not only their responsibility, since you allow them to. If you let them continue doing it to you, you will not be transformed. Resolve the practice of repressing and oppressing that arises out of fear, of bitterness and sadness.

The more you are in contact with your deep feeling and identify what you are really feeling, the greater your capacity and ability will be to change your negative internal programming and improve your inner dialogue.

It is good that you allow yourself to feel without preventing your feelings and emotions from expressing themselves. Feeling and accepting the emotions that appear without trying to avoid them acts as a liberator of your repressed parts, which may have been blocked for a long time.

Another factor that we should consider is what we give from our heart to others. Let us have a heart that does not give sorrow. A heart that does not consume sorrow. This is also important, because, when sorrow enters the heart, the soul feels trapped by its own grief and cannot dance in the light of its being, it cannot be grateful, and enters into the dynamic of the complaint, the lament and grief. A heart into which sorrow has entered causes sorrow to others since that is what it gives.

The majority of times we allow suffering to enter into the heart through words that we have heard, and the person who said them did not have the intention of hurting us, but we 'consume' it. That is what habits are like. Then, to protect the heart, we close it in a defense system that is bad for it, since it leaves no room to breathe.

True protection comes from inner wisdom. Of knowing that everything is relative and that words are not infallible, the wind carries them off; don't let's accumulate them with grief, like thorns inside us.

Let us have a heart from which healing love emanates, love that joins broken hearts (it patches them together). Don't let us be one of those people who with their words and attitudes break their hearts and that of others. Let us have a heart of light and not one of steel. Light cannot be cut by a knife nor scratched by a stone. It is free.

Life is to be felt.

THE BODY

We keep feelings rooted in our body, experiences that we had in the past, and that we haven't known how to let go of, understand, listen to, or heal. The body keeps these feelings alive so that you can listen to them and receive their message. Independently of what you have lived or are living through, don't ask why, but rather, what for?

All the things that have happened to you relate to one another and are inspired in (and connected to) a higher purpose. Listen to your body and you will realize that they have meaning. You will see.

I am not going to go into this subject in depth. There are many books written on transformation in relation to listening to illness and the signs that the body gives out. Many people have experienced a personal transformation after an accident or an illness.

3

Intuition

In this chapter we will see how to approach our intuition in order to listen to it, understand it and use it in our life.
We will see the following sections:
The key of intuition
Accessing the information
The heart has reasons that the reason does not understand
Intuition is felt
Connecting with the inner teacher
Why don't we listen to intuition?

The key of intuition

Our intuition is key to our personal creativity. It can help us to keep going in moments of uncertainty. It connects us to our inner compass.

In life there are many situations for which no one gives you a recipe. It is your own intuition and your decision of that moment which saves you from an accident or protects you from a negative influence. It is that inner voice that whispers to you in those moments to help you to decide.

With the intuition you don't enter into the process of analyzing, doubting, intellectualizing, questioning. Because of this, in situations of uncertainty and chaos, it helps you. With the intuition you make a rapid and precise evaluation. It is like seeing it and clicking. That's it!

If you react to chaos with the automatic pilot of your habits and customs — complaints, anger, resistance, lack of acceptance, correction, it should be different, etc. — the intuition does not work because:

- You get too involved.
- You consider yourself the savior.
- You try to fix it and it gets worse.
- You don't keep clarity.
- You choose sides, you lose your equanimity.
- There is too much noise and movement inside you and you cannot hear the voice of intuition.

Different voices speak to you: the voice of your ego, the one influenced by your past, by the people you depend on or who you value or are attached to, the voice of others' opinion, that of your desires; that of your logic and the voice of your intuition connected to your conscience. Sometimes they all speak to you at the same time: which do you listen to? How do you decide? Your mind goes from one channel to another and this confuses you even more.

We call the capacity to use and understand the creative inner language intuition. Eric Rolf describes it thus: "Life talks to each person in such a simple way that we can all understand it: it talks to us directly or through metaphors. Personal intuition, the one that we each have, is the instrument to interpret it with."

Introversion helps you to connect to your essence. In that inner connection intuition emerges and you learn to differentiate it from your ego and from all the voices that accompany it.

We have different channels that our mind functions through. We are dispersed over many subjects. We think about our wife or our husband, our lover, our child or children or the grandchildren, our project, our job, what happened or is to happen, money, the car or the boat, the meeting, the post, the Blackberry, the weekend, the holidays, our parents, etc. We jump from one channel to another without centering ourselves. We are dispersed over many subjects.

When we manage to be present, HERE AND NOW, we are people with great potential, a lot of strength. All of our energy and our strength are HERE. Our intuition and creativity align with our purpose and generosity, and what we do has an impact, it renews, it generates trust and hope.

In order to be present, we develop the habit of stopping, reflecting, silencing. In the silence we get back strength, we let ideas take hold and we learn to trust in our intuition. Then we act from the heart of our being. Our responses arise out of love and trust and not of fear, clinging or bitterness.

The wisdom of our intuition offers us a true guide. How often do we have an intuition to do something but our logic, our mind, our beliefs, say to us: "No, no, not this way, that way." Afterwards you think: "I should have done what I intuited." We don't trust in this intuition because there are a lot of mixtures of selfishness, fears, opinions, voices.

A sure intuition that manifests itself at least with relative frequency implies and supposes a solid intellectual and spiritual development, as well as maturity and emotional intelligence. Or, if not, it can wander off to the region of fantasy.

The intuition is the thread between the personal and the universal, the diverse and the one, the material and the spirit; it is the understanding of what beauty is, what certainty is and what creativity is; what power is and what serenity is; what is permanence and what is discovery.

The intuition is the strength of the pioneer, the inspiration of the genius, the splendor of the creator, both in Art and Science, in Religion and Philosophy, in Politics or in any other field that an effort can be made towards knowledge, for progress, for creativity, for perfecting and for service to the general good. An enormous list of the greatest figures in the history of humanity has left it expressly confirmed that intuition was the inspiring light that opened the way towards the most important of their works.

To become truly intuitive is the result of a long and persistent evolutionary effort that presupposes a great previous personal, spiritual, mental, intellectual and emotional development, not only on concrete levels but also in the more subtle ones.

The intuition is the faculty of an awakened consciousness: it allows you to become aware, have a global vision that is connected to spiritual intelligence.

It is important for our spirit to soar in flight. Wayne Dyer comments in one of his books that two kinds of people exist: ducks and eagles. The ducks go through life as victims and do nothing except complain (whatever the reality they find themselves facing). The eagles, on the contrary, take the initiative and fly much higher than the crowd. Not because they are superior or want to separate themselves, but because they connect to their essential truths and they are awake, they enjoy all their potential and the greatness and marvel of nature.

Potentially we are all eagles, since true power is within us. **It is not a question of filling oneself from the outside in, but of recovering that energy, that inner strength, aligning consciousness with decision, word and action**. It is a question of aligning reason and intuition, mind and heart. How do we readjust our dispersed energies to have that inner power and that alignment? Meditating, we find harmony with the center of our being. Meditation helps us to create the habit of responding out of serenity and being aware. Let's reflect, let's meditate, let's pause on the road and observe.

Accessing the information

The intuition gives a direct access, not going through the rational, to information about which we are not normally aware. It is the capacity that we have to know something without a logical base. You know something without knowing how you know it; you intuit it and you are right.

The intuition opens us to a new channel of information that allows us to be more aligned, more in contact with our soul, and to listen inside and outside of our body, to everything that is around us.

You have had an intuitive experience when you have accessed information that is not 'yours', that is, when you know something that you have never learned, discovered, experienced or lived consciously and, it seems, that information is correct.

Limiting beliefs do not allow you to listen to your intuition; they block you. We tend to deny our possibilities and to limit our potential. **Intuition is not thought; it is listened to.** To think is to seek and to listen is to find.

We use intuition to access a level of consciousness different to that which maintains the problem. It has already been said by Einstein: a problem cannot be resolved with the same level of consciousness that creates it.

The heart has reasons that the reason does not understand

Intuition is a direct channel of communication with our inner self. It comes from the heart of the soul. What brakes its expression is the head, the logical and rational part. Our logic is limited. We try to go in a straight line. The only straight lines that exist in the Universe are those that man has created.

An intuition, if you follow it, is gentle when it appears. If you repress it, when it finally expresses itself it can appear in the form of a passionate impulse, compulsive and it can even become destructive. Not to pay attention to intuitions is like turning your back on life.

Intuition is felt

Intuition is felt, it is not thought, although what is felt is then turned into thought. The greater part of our thoughts is about the past, but **intuition is always of the present moment**. Any rational process in order to make a decision takes time and a lot of thinking energy. Intuitive decisions are instantaneous and almost don't need energy.

Following an intuition is sometimes called **following your heart**. You have a feeling and you follow it without analyzing, without needing a reason.

Many inventors, scientists, entrepreneurs, researchers, etc. explain to us how they have reached their best decisions and greatest inspirations intuitively, while they were in a relaxed place. In an environment where the noisy, chatty, doubt-generating mind is calm enough to allow the self to listen to that voice and feel those subtle feelings in the heart. Only then does the ego stand to one side. The ego is always interested in sabotaging and distorting intuitions. In that moment, on standing to one side, a clear path is opened so that the intuition can appear – the messenger in our conscious awareness.

In a world where we learn to cover over, hide, protect, defend and attack, we build barriers around us and in ourselves in such a way that our subtle intuitive sense has more difficulties in doing its work.

Our intuitions are essentially messages from the heart, Mike George explains to us; not our physical heart, but our spiritual heart. That is why very few have developed this intuitive faculty. Our education is almost totally focused around the memory, thoughts about memories, processes of the reason and structures of rationality. On a mental level, this brings with it a lot of noise. A constantly thinking mind is a noisy mind. Unless the self understands and sees this, the attention of the self is continuously distracted by the mental conversation and is incapable of listening to and feeling the feelings of the heart. This mental stimulation can easily turn into an addiction.

Einstein said: "The intuitive mind is a sacred gift and the rational mind is a faithful servant. We have created a society that honors the society and has forgotten the gift."

Connecting to our inner teacher

Intuition helps us to pick up on signals through a place, a person, an atmosphere, a vibration. However, the deepest form of intuition is not the one that connects us to external energies, but rather that which reconnects us with our inner energy. This energy can be called wisdom or truth. It lives in the heart of our consciousness (our spiritual heart) and it speaks to us at each moment of our life. It reminds us of **the true meaning of** *intuition* —**inner tutor**—. It is our teacher and our guide and also our lover, given that it is love, because the deepest truth is that we are love, and the deepest guide in life is love (not romantic love, Hollywood-style).

Why don't we listen to intuition?

This leads us to asking ourselves: if the existence of this truth, this wisdom, this love, in the same heart of our being is real... why don't we listen to it, and why don't we let ourselves be guided by it? And when we listen to it, why don't we trust in it easily? The simple answer is: because of our rational material programming.

We are programmed to believe that life is a journey and a lineal, rational and physical process. And that we need a lot of mental energy on the road. We are programmed to believe that any matter or problem that surfaces in our life requires a lot of thought on a rational level. And that our thinking should be guided and measured by the rational theories of others, their formulas and models (education). That way we get lost in the thinking and negate our access to the inner wisdom that lies in our hearts.

On stifling the small inner voice with mental and rational chatter, we annul the subtle feelings and cover over the guiding and wise light of our heart, what in other words we call the voice of intuition. Then we either don't listen to the intuition, we ignore it or we give it a wide berth. As a result, there is a poverty of wisdom in our present-day world; there is usually a lack of real love in our relationships and we often live lives designed for utilitarianism, without our soul being in them; they are functional and without the spark of happiness and daily enjoyment.

4

How to Live Creatively in a Chaotic World

In this chapter we will reflect on our responsibility to create, allowing the old pillars holding up the old paradigm to collapse.

We will see how it is important to keep our purpose and act in times of uncertainty.

We will reflect upon why the creativity that we have does not lead us to the transformation that we want? Why does the energy not rise?

The chapter ends with the section 'Going to the other shore', that is, definitively leaving behind the shore of darkness in order to go to the shore where the self shines in its wholeness.

The sections you will find in this chapter are:
Living creatively in a chaotic world
Keeping the purpose
In uncertainty, act
Why does the creativity that we have not lead us to the transformation that we want? Why does the energy not rise?
Going to the other shore

Living creatively in a chaotic world

In the twenty-first century we are exposed to living many unexpected situations; unexpected and sudden in their occurrence. Others we see coming but when they arrive, we touch rock bottom, they disconcert us, they break us. We feel whipped around by being fired, illnesses, accidents, separations, sudden deaths, explosions and an endless amount of events that cause unhappiness, conflict, pain and anger. We hurry to seek guilty parties in order to project onto them our sorrows and our anger.

The worldwide ego-system is destined to die, it is unsustainable; its pillars are collapsing. It seems that the society of consumption and well-being that we have created is falling on top of us little by little. Some still don't see it. It needs courage to see and recognize it.

Awakening and seeing, seeing and awakening, helps us to be aware of the following questions:

- What is happening?
- Where are we going?
- What is my responsibility and yours?
- What do I have to do NOW?

To answer these four questions in depth requires another book to be written. Answering them in essence I can say that the pillars of avarice, greed, the ego and pride can no longer uphold the market based on what *I* want, where *I* become more powerful and more visible, more famous, more dominant, richer, and not on what is better for others and for the world.

We are moving towards a collapse of the ego-system.

We are moving towards a clearing-up of the elements of nature that no longer can put up with the pollution, violence and mistreatment. Eckhart Tolle explains it clearly: "Since human life and human consciousness are intrinsically one with the life of the planet, as the old consciousness dissolves, there are bound to be synchronistic geographical and climatic natural upheavals in many parts of the planet, some of which we are already witnessing now."

We are going towards a new world. If we want to. If we take responsibility. If we begin NOW.

Our responsibility is to allow these pillars of the ego-system to collapse and disappear first in our beings and in our lives. Let us create out of a new awareness from spaces of generosity, abundance, opening and love. Spaces about which I will speak in the chapter, 'The Space that Creativity Bursts Forth From' (see page 115).

Let us act out of an awakened consciousness. While this new consciousness emerges on the planet and in each one of us, the old one is dissolving. The ego is more and more dysfunctional, things do not work however many patches we try to put over them; the old system is cracking and it is collapsing.

We have lived mirages as if they were real, unsustainable lifestyles as if they were sustainable. The curtains are opening and reality is emerging.

You can despair, get depressed, writhe with pain. Or you can choose to see, awaken, be aware and act.

When the caterpillar no longer functions as a caterpillar and it can no longer drag itself along or eat to get fat, it goes into its cocoon and goes through a chaotic metamorphosis. Its shape is transformed, and while it does this, it needs:

- To be inside.
- To go with the process, that is, not to block it. To give itself up to it.
- To dare to let go of its old shape, to die in order to be reborn.
- To have patience.
- Perseverance.

These are the qualities that we need to go through our metamorphosis.

Keeping the purpose

In the uncertainty of these chaotic moments of personal and worldwide metamorphosis, we need to be clear about our purpose. I will deal with this at more length in the chapter: Transformative Creativity, in the section 'Creativity in one's purpose' (see page 57).

For many, the purpose continues to be of the old paradigm:

- Maintaining the status quo.
- Having a house near the sea or in the mountains.
- Having one's own company.
- An inflated image of oneself:
  - Being a rich business person,
  - Being a famous author, or,
  - That one's ideas are those that are imposed onto others.
- Having a few hundred thousand in the bank.

The purposes of this kind do not give real power. They maintain the culture of the ego-system and continue to generate stress, pressure, pain, poverty, injustice, corruption, illness and imbalance. They create and maintain chaos.

We should make sure to channel our purpose towards emerging and being out of our authenticity. It will be a dynamic and energetic purpose aimed at global change and not at satisfying our own ego. It will be a purpose that will arise out of spaces of abundance and generosity, silence and enthusiasm. We will be like Vishnu: bestowers connected to the essence (see page 92).

When we maintain our purpose in our consciousness, the power of the intention acts with force: you create what you believe. The desires and the intentions can change the physical manifestation of reality.

In uncertainty, act

- Act out of the space of emptiness and silence (see pages 124 and 127).
- Don't let panic take over. Remember that everything is fine. Everything is as it is. Accept it.
- Trust.
- Don't let yourself be overly impressed. Go with the wave as the surfer does, don't let it drown you. Play with it and keep yourself afloat. When something or someone overly

impresses you, you allow it or them to dominate you and you lose the connection with yourself. You lower your value and your strength.

- Be consistent to your principles. Don't let yourself be influenced by opinions that arise out of people's ego-character and those who are afraid of 'losing' something. Fear of losing any of the seven Ps (see page 46). With your transformation, you turn into their mirror and, as they do not wish to see, they will try to convince you.
- Act for the good of all. Include, do not exclude. Unite, don't separate. Don't act only for *your* group, *your* community, *your* religion, *your* country, but rather so that consciousness might awaken and emerge in all human beings and for the benefit of all. Have the world in your vision. Your presence and acts have an influence
- Believe in yourself.

Why does the creativity that we have not lead us to the transformation that we want? Why does the energy not rise?

- We carry on creating out of our selfishness.
- We create more of the same.
- We create out of our smallness: we get stuck in the scene and stop seeing the global perspective.
- We have big ideas that come from selfish consciousnesses, closed spaces, broken, crushed suffering hearts.
- We create out of a space of need.
- We carry on blindly.
- We stay in hypocrisy, focused on material needs and then everything is superficial.
- We do not ask ourselves the fundamental questions that will change our perception, our experience of things, of the self and of relationships.

We Stay In Laziness

- Lazy intellects get lost in action.
- Lazy minds do not take on the responsibility for creating their destiny.
- Lazy minds depend on being entertained and consume the creativity of the other.
- Laziness destroys the capacity to innovate. We cannot talk of the true newness.
- Laziness takes you to a state of degenerative inactivity in which carelessness takes control of you, you stop taking risks and living with passion.
- Laziness can come with the attitude of *I* already know. With the pride that arises out of believing that one already knows, you pay less attention to continuing to learn, you close off to new learning.
- There isn't any enthusiasm. The being gets weaker.

Stabilize yourself in your form of inner power and go forward from there. Don't let laziness absorb you and reduce your light. In the next chapters you will find methods to achieve it.

We Sustain Violence

Violence is re-creative, it moves energy, and provokes the adrenaline to which so many are addicted.

Violence is destructive. It destroys order, existence and nature. It destroys the peace, it breaks hearts and it dries up their love.

Violence:

- damages,
- divides,
- breaks,
- submits,
- represses,

- oppresses,
- kills, and,
- exhausts.

We are so addicted that we do not see. And, if we do see, the addiction is such that it does not allow us to act in accordance with what we see. As we need our dosage of adrenaline in order to feel ourselves to be alive, we get used to it. And we continue in the old paradigm. Tolle says to us: "Driven by greed, ignorant of their connectedness to the whole, human beings persist in a behavior that, if continued unchecked, can only result in their own destruction."

Going to the other shore

Let us learn to go to the other shore. Let us cut the moorings that tie us to laziness, greed, violence, selfish comfort and let us begin the journey in the boat of truth. The truth will make you free, the Bible tells us. And the *Upanishads* say: "If you do not feel free, it is only because you are not true."

- Let us leave the shore of our sorrow to go to happiness, bliss, enjoyment, well-being, wholeness.
- Let us leave the shore of our loneliness, let us go to feel ourselves included in the wonder of the Creator and creation.
- Let us leave the shore of our stress and lack of tranquility, let us go to the shore of peace, harmony and presence.
- Let us leave the shore of our inner noise, let us go to the shore of the silence of the essence of the self.

Get onto the boat and let the purest energy of the Universe, the divine presence, flow through you and be in you. He is the boatman. Give yourself up to His love. Surrender to His light and let go of the moorings. He will take care of the rest. Trust.

5

Transformative Creativity

The past does not have power over you.

Creativity is the great ally of transformation. In the process of trans-formation, fears, resistances and blockages appear. With creativity you vanquish them, you dissolve them and you overcome them.

In this chapter we will see the importance of centering yourself on your point of power: the power of now. We will look briefly at the subject of blockages in organizations and resistances to change.

In order to live through the process of transformation successfully you need to be the leader of your life. So the next section is centered on moving towards self-leadership. One of the factors that interferes in your personal leadership is getting attached to and clinging on to what you create. You confuse the creator – you – with your creation. We will see this in the section entitled 'Your expression'.

The key to transforming is in knowing how to forget and how to remember. I will deal with this in 'The power of RE-REmembering' (You recognize, You return, You re-link, Religion, You restore, Resurrection, You renew, You reinvent, You rejuvenate).

Balance is necessary in order for us not to go off track and go against what we ourselves want. That is why balance between analyzing and feeling is necessary.

Other tools that help us to be inspired, that act as an incentive and drive us to transform ourselves are in the power to return to your archetype, and understanding the personality types and what yours is concretely. We will see this in 'Returning to your archetype': the six Greek goddesses, the eight Hindu Shaktis and the personality types.

We will see the difference between change, transformation and metamorphosis in the section on 'Levels of transformation'.

To transform yourself it is not enough to be creative, you need to have an attractive future aim that is greater than the cost of the change. What is the incentive for the transformation? Once you are clear about your purpose, you need to be creative in order to apply it and live it out in your daily life. We will look at this in 'Creativity in one's purpose'. The subheadings you will find in this chapter are:

- *Transformative creativity*
- *The power of now*
- *Blockages in organizations*
- *Resistances to change*
- *Towards a self-leadership*
- *Your expression*
- *The power of RE-REmembering*
- *Balance between analyzing and feeling*
- *Returning to your archetype*
- *The personality types*
- *Levels of transformation*
- *What is the incentive for transformation?*
- *Creativity in one's purpose*

Transformative creativity

When our dream breaks, the horizon is shattered, the pillars on which our life was based collapse. We are disappointed. It is the moment to reinvent ourselves.

Do not ignore the possibilities that you have. Discover your inner resources. It is a great opportunity. Some doors close. It is the moment to open others and begin a new stage without regret. Let go of the past. Accept the present.

Look through the window and observe all the possibilities, seeing beyond where you are now. Get out of the cage of your limitations. Without fear. Trust. The Universe will send you help.

Build a bridge that joins the place where you are with the place you want to go to. Begin to walk over the bridge walking from the NOW to the future self. Don't let anything anchor you to the past. Go forward.

Past is past. Events happened and now they are past. What remains is the impression that they left on you. You can change those memories by modifying your way of seeing the events of the past, widening the context, the painting you have placed yourself in. You can recognize the learning experiences. You can forgive and let go. That way you change the reading that you make of your past; you stop carrying a burden. You free yourself and are grateful for what the experiences have brought you in life.

The power of now

The transforming process begins in the present, which is our point of power. In the present we choose, we create the future and we change the past. We cannot change the facts, but we can change our version of them, and this has a greater value than changing the facts, given that these are more real inside us as metaphors than as facts in themselves.

Each moment is new. Each moment in life is a new start as you distance yourself from the old. This instant is a new point of departure for you, here and now.

In order to do something different, you have to be different.

It is having a vital catalyzing attitude of lasting transformation. It is taking risks. It is getting back for good the shine in your heart and your eyes.

You have the answer in front of you; to see it you have to be present in the present.

Anthony Strano reminds us that:

Contentment comes and only comes
When I decide to live as I am meant to live.
To be what I know I am,
To love others as they are,
To be attentive to the needs of now.

Blockages in organizations

Sometimes, as managers, leaders or people who manage teams, we have the difficulty of trusting in our collaborators, of giving them projects that are of interest, of providing them with challenges, of delegating. There we find the same old fears. And the higher you are in the organization, the more panic sets in, since there is more to lose.

Let's maintain the status quo as much as we can! It appears as the paradigm of survival and thus we observe the conservative style of the organizations that generally allow for the 'breaking up of nothing', not even though everything around us is breaking up. In the coaching sessions that I am giving to managers of a multinational company that has 250,000 employees, some of them have commented to me how the fear of the boss blocks any initiative, and this does not allow for the taking of risks nor generating changes.

To generate changes in organizations, the people who comprise them have to be prepared to change. Not only change the language and appearance, but change the culture, the background and the way of doing things. Changing the pillars that hold up beliefs and attitudes, and changing intentions. The managers should be leaders who serve if they want to participate in creating a sustainable system.

Resistances to change

In the crisis, we see what I call the 7 Ps under threat. The crisis means changes. In the face of the changes let us observe our responses. As I write in my book *Live in Freedom*: "When an important change takes place in your life, observe your response. If you resist accepting change it is because you are afraid. Afraid of losing something. Perhaps you might lose your position, a property, possession or money. Change might mean that you lose privileges or prestige. Perhaps with change you lose closeness to a person or a place."

We can cling to our lifestyle, our privileges.

In life, all these things, summarized in the seven Ps (position, property, pay, privileges, prestige, person and place), come and go and then others appear which will also go. It is like a river in constant movement. If we try to stop the flow of the river, we create a damn; the water stagnates and causes a pressure which accumulates inside us. We live under the pressure of time, of deadlines, of what has to be done, but above all the pressure that we feel at the fear of what might happen, the fear of what we could lose or are already losing.

We can act out of fear, insecurity, attachment, clinging. Because we are afraid of losing. Because we base our self-esteem on power, on privileges, on our properties. Losing them supposes a threat to our self-esteem.

In the face of this dynamic of human behavior we need trust, creativity and courage. To go within, to know how to reflect, and stop looking for guilty parties outside of us. To take on responsibility and to know how to let go. All that we really need will come to find us; we don't have to cling on to it.

Towards self-leadership

The great fundamental values that give meaning and content to our life do not depend on our privileges, possessions, role or properties. They will depend on our intelligence, our awareness and acting in an aligned way, on being coherent and whole in what we think, say or do.

Perhaps we should learn to let go, to not grab, to allow to flow; that is, to live without resistances, being creators of constructive changes that bring about improvements and widen our horizons. To have this capacity of creative and positive response it is necessary to balance action with introversion, silence, reflection and meditation. We achieve mastery in life when our action is balanced with reflection and is strengthened by silence.

That way we begin the path of self-leadership. We cannot

exercise true leadership over others if we are not capable of leading our own mind, emotions and inner world. If we want to sleep and our worries do not allow us to. If we determine to do sport or exercise but we don't do it. If we care little for our body. If we think in a jumbled way. This lack of personal leadership prevents us from exercising a true leadership.

When we lead out of trust, we open up and promote creativity and innovation. To create spaces of trust means to let people take risks, not to be afraid of getting it wrong, to dare to show initiative knowing that they will be supported. When we manage to lead our life like that, we inspire a creative and transforming movement around us and in others.

Your expression

Transformative creativity is a creativity without attachment to the expression of the self. When you identify yourself with the expression you attach yourself and live through it. That takes away from your authenticity. On identifying yourself with the expression you lose what is genuine; you are possessive of it. I am not the painting I paint, nor the book that I write. Although we transmit what we are and what we feel through the word and expression, to identify ourselves with it makes us become possessive and limits us.

If you create a work of art, allow it to have its own life.

If you create a child, allow it to live its own life.

You even have to learn not to attach yourself to your own emotions which are your creation. See them relatively. Don't identify with them. They are your creation, you are their creator; you are not the creation.

If you are attached to an emotion, as you express yourself, your words will not be clear to the other person, the receiver of them. There is a mixture, and it is difficult to understand the message, as the words say one thing, the emotion another and your attachment interferes with the transmission. When you speak from your being, your message is clear. That is, you aren't narcissistic. Your life is not centered only on yourself.

For transformation, you begin with a seed which is you: you go inwards in order to cleanse and nourish yourself. We have thorns inside, such as anger, negativity, bitterness, disappointment, pain. We have to go from the thorn to the seed, where all our potential for healing and liberating love is to be found.

We nourish the seed and we grow, we connect to the highest energy and vibration, we go upwards. And, as a result, our being flourishes. The flower emerges from the seed; it needs a stimulus, but once it receives it, it grows naturally. Thus, on flowering, we transmit our color, our fragrance and we share our fruits. That is, we go outside of ourselves: we serve. Thus do we become an offering to others.

The power of RE-REmembering

We go from the thorn to the seed by remembering. With the memory we return to our essence, we make the memory of our essential being emerge. The capacity to forget and to remember are two extraordinary faculties that we have. If we know how to use them, we will reach wholeness. Do not forget what you have to remember. Do not remember what you have to forget.

With the REmembering, you:

REcognize your originality, your awakened consciousness.
REturn to the original, to your spiritual origin.
REjoin, that is, you connect to your divine self and to God. The word Religion arises out of the Latin term REligare.
REturn to your beauty.
REstore your identity.
RElease falsity, what is not yours, until you forget it because it does not belong to you.
REnew and you REinvent yourself.
REjuvenate: your energy flows creatively.

With all of this, you experience a REsurrection: you are born again to the brilliance of your being. That is, you offer something unique to others that comes from the authenticity of your being. The Garden of Eden is made up of people. Each one offers something unique of themselves.

In reality — Anthony Strano tells us —,

I only have what I truly am,
that is my strength.
If I have borrowed power from a name,
a role, a position, a group or a person,
there comes a point when it all dissolves
and I will feel empty.
Floundering for a sense of identity and
desperate for self-esteem.
I decide to go 'inside' to find myself,
Wisdom and solutions are already there.
Simply I need to remember.

Balance between analyzing and feeling

If you reach your point of truth, in your being, when you express it, it comes out naturally. It is not a huge effort nor is it laborious. We need synthesis and a little analytical effort. We have to find a point of balance. If we go beyond that point, things go in the opposite direction than we want them to.

For example, we see what happens with determination: if you are not careful, it makes you intense and rigid, then you force things and impose. Doing so you cause an opposite reaction and a greater resistance which opposes what it is that you want to achieve. It is to make a bad use of that quality. Another example is when we expand ourselves too much in our words: it is easy for us to go off track and get diverted from the path, distancing ourselves from the essence. We talk a lot and we say little. We misuse the power of the word and then it loses power.

If you are too emotional or too intellectual, you don't find the point where you have to stop. There is a point at which the emotions or intellectualization have to stop. If you are capable of placing a limit on it and of stopping, then you can transcend this limit; thus gaining access to the experience of the awareness of the soul.

The people that analyze a lot or who are very emotional and do not find their balance have greater difficulties in reaching their center, their being, inner silence. When they try to meditate, they get lost in their mental analysis or in the strength of their emotions.

We need the intellect in order to understand peace, speak of peace, analyze peace, to then transcend intellectualization and analysis and go to experience, enter into feeling the peace, personifying peace.

It is important not to get stuck in your intelligence, wit or intellectual sharpness, as this blocks gentleness, kindness and tenderness. You believe that you already know, and with the 'I already know' you do not leave an opening space. Look for paths to feel, reconcile, bring harmony and be kind.

It is important not to identify with your emotions and get lost in them. With so much 'feeling', you don't reason, and wisdom stays blocked.

Each person has to find their balance between reason and feeling. Not go to extremes.

An anonymous mystic of the fourteenth century already advised us of this in his book *The Cloud of Unknowing*:

Our intense need to understand will always be a powerful stumbling block to our attempts to reach God in simple love [...] and must always be overcome. For if you do not overcome this need to understand, it will undermine your quest. It will replace the darkness which you have pierced to reach God with clear images of something which, however good, however beautiful, however Godlike, is not God.

And so I urge you, go after experience rather than knowledge. On account of pride, knowledge may often deceive you, but this gentle, loving affection will not deceive you. Knowledge tends to breed conceit, but love builds. Knowledge is full of labor, but love, full of rest.

Another tool that can help you in transformative creativity is understanding your archetype and/or your enneatype.

Returning to your archetype

The archetype is the print, the design, the original code. A code made up of non-violence, harmony, unity, respect, love, peace and the being that dances in the pure light of its freedom. Returning to this original code frees you from the tendencies to depend, dominate, defend and fear. You get back your self-esteem.

The archetypes usually have a spiritual origin. They manifest qualities that are not violent or selfish; nor do they create suffering.

This is not a book about archetypes. But it seemed important to me to mention them, as images of wisdom to which we can have access through remembering, with the power of the RE.

Different archetypes can be used: the warrior, the hermit, the hero, the pilgrim, the master...

We can look to the **six Greek goddesses**:

Athena: goddess of wisdom. She kept her virginity. She helped humanity in her peace-making works.

Artemis: goddess of purity and protector of the innocent. Goddess of the moon.

Hestia: goddess of family peace. Carer. She is the most gentle and tender of all.

Demeter: mother, the goddess of agriculture, of fertility, the mother deity associated with the earth. The goddess of the birth of the world: the flowers, fruits and other living things were the gifts of Demeter.

Hera: patron goddess of the family and of married women.

Aphrodite: goddess of beauty and love. Patron of love and of lovers.

There are also the eight Hindu goddesses, **the eight Shaktis**. Let us awaken the sleeping Shakti that we carry within:

Lakshmi: goddess of wealth, the archetype of the power to co-operate that comes from all the powers together. She embodies beauty, harmony and unity.

Durga: archetype of the power to let go. She destroys defects. With the weapons of knowledge and detachment, she embodies the pure and true. She breaks with the illusory and the mirages.

Sarasvati: goddess of truth. She has wisdom and an intellect capable of deciding in action. She has a function of education and of conceding the capacity to free oneself of submission through the clarity of decision based on practical wisdom.

Kali: archetype of the power to confront; she has courage and audacity. She protects the home from deceased spirits. Her integrity without failings allows her to break the chains that imprison the soul and distance her from her original innocence and from God.

Jagadamba: archetype of the power to love and tolerate. With that power she is considered to be the mother of the world. She overflows with love, and with her love she heals the pain of hearts and she touches them with divine love.

Santoshima: archetype of the power to adapt oneself. Her power consists of transforming adverse situations into rich and stimulating events. She smiles constantly. She has the capacity to give space to the preferences, opinions and needs of others. With her trident she destroys the opinions rooted in the ego.

Parvati: archetype of the power to center oneself, the power that offers a new perspective, clarity and calm. She offers the clarity to change a situation. She has her own autonomous identity. She appreciates solitude and is able to extract herself momentarily from the world that surrounds her to be able to perceive and understand better.

Gayatri: archetype of the power to discern. She is the capacity to use the intellect with the art of consulting her own most conscious self, in order to discern the authentic from the false, the good from the bad, the reality from the illusory, what is beneficial and what brings with it a loss.

The personality types

Another useful connection to put transformative creativity into action can be done with the personality types through the enneatypes of the Enneagram. They help us to know ourselves and to understand what our essence is. They help us to realize when we are in the ego character, far from our virtue and the ill that this does to us.

The nine enneatypes are: the inspector, the assistant, the administrator, the author or artist, the wise one, the facilitator, the optimist, the leader (the boss or the champion) and the negotiator (different authors give them different names).

Some people have more of one tendency and others another, but the qualities can be combined. For example, one goes more towards wisdom, another towards purity; one is more of the head and another of the heart. The enneatypes show us the combinations that complement us, strengthen us and make us whole, and which, on the contrary, disintegrate us and unbalance us.

It is a question of reconnecting to your original self and working from there to eliminate the patterns of negative behavior. This reconnection allows you to deal with and transform those acquired patterns and habits.

The base for personal transformation is in REturning to the original, genuine and imperishable. To the essence of your being. Practice the power of the RE!

You cannot transform yourself if you only concentrate on the bad, on the weak. Only if you concentrate on your original goodness do you connect to your inner strength and come out of the cage of negativity; you enter into the beauty of being, you widen horizons, you unfold your wings, you fly and your being in freedom expresses itself as a gift to the world.

Levels of transformation

When we talk of change and transformation, we are dealing with different levels. We can change the furniture around, but we haven't made a true transformation. We continue in the same space, with the same furniture. Sometimes we do the same with our feelings; we change them around inside us, we put them in another place, but we continue to have them inside.

We can consider three levels:

- Change:
- It is more external and temporal
- It is to change the place of things. Or change the place or partner but at bottom we continue with the same elements; although there is an external change, our patterns of behavior continue.
- External change can facilitate transformation because it forces us to break certain internal circuits. However, habits are strong and true transformation lies in breaking them. With external change it is not enough.

- Transformation:
- It is internal and it manifests on the outside.
- It is to heal, to learn, to forgive and let go.
- It is to leave the inner prison definitively, creating a new mentality. In the transformation we have made the effort of breaking with the custom of being what we thought we were to let the true self emerge. We have overcome

temptations, resistances, tensions.
- It is to transform the force of the excess into empathy, understanding and compassion.

- Metamorphosis:
- META MOR PHOSIS, in Greek, means that the form has changed.
- It is lasting.
- It is a total and definitive transformation. There is no going back.

In metamorphosis you enter into the cocoon of healing love and silence. There is then such a metamorphosis that when you come out others see you and don't recognize you any more. You have transformed so much that your old self has died. You have freed yourself. You have let the ego die. You have practiced the aphorism of the *Upanishads* which says: "The divine vision radiates out from the lack of ego." Unless the seed dies, the tree is not born. The ego has to dissolve for the Divine to manifest Itself. The Divine is the best insurance, but Its price is high: the ego.

What is the incentive for transformation?

We live our reality and also find our answers according to the questions we ask. Sometimes the answer is of pain, sadness and disappointment. The questions lead us to anchor ourselves in the past, not to live learning in the present or generating a constant transformation.

Let us look at some factors which are incentives for transformation:

- You are encouraged to transform yourself by the question: why am I going to stay stuck here, in this stress, in these bitter feelings, in this emptiness and without achievements? Why am I going to continue with these recurrent experiences that repeat themselves again and again?

- Wanting to leave stress behind. When the pain becomes unsustainable, I am prepared to leave it.
- When there is a loss, a limit situation, you feel obliged to transform.
- Wanting to heal the past: healing forms part of transformation.
- The immediate thing is perhaps to want to leave suffering behind, but underneath there is a feeling of wanting to get one's dignity back. The feeling of having a natural, not selfish, right, to live with one's personal worth. It is a call to personal dignity. Why am I going to continue to be like a cabbage? It is a call that I feel to the right to happiness. The right to express myself. The right to be myself.
- Asking oneself: why isn't my life going as I want it to? Do I experience the desired results? If the answer is NO, we should revise our inner programming: perceptions, beliefs and memories that block our progress, always without looking for outside guilty parties, or if not, we won't transform anything.
- The 'collapse', the 'final blow', reaching a limit situation in which you can put up with no more.
- The 'creative' suffering does not destroy but rather, in that suffering, you go through the dark night of the soul, through the desert in which you let go of many things and you are transformed.
- The dissatisfaction of the present moment pushes you to seek a change. The threshold of dissatisfaction that is necessary to begin transformation is different for everyone.
- Realizing that you create your own reality.
- Out of love towards yourself, towards others and the world, you feel the need and the responsibility to transform yourself.

Creativity in one's purpose

In transformative creativity, purpose is essential. Once you find your purpose, it is necessary to be creative to live it out. In the book *Live in Freedom* I deal with re-finding your purpose, methods and paths to facilitate it.

It is important to re-find the meaning of what you do, what you do it for and for whom. If not, what happens is that you connect to the forms, the laws, the external, the labels. And you get lost. You turn into an automaton.

On staying connected to your purpose, you make your purpose more creative. The purpose is usually linked to the best of you, with expressing and sharing it. It is on giving and sharing that we find our wholeness.

In any case, we cannot jump towards the purpose of a broad and unlimited life without taking the necessary steps for it. The small steps are crucial. Each day, select a purpose. It might be to do with how you treat people in your job, your family or yourself. Give yourself a daily purpose, such as for example:

- Being better at work.
- Being better with my children.
- Being better with my parents.
- Being better with myself, in me, for me.
- Today I am going to look at things with more optimism.

They don't have to be heroic purposes; they can be inviting your friends to have a cup of tea, creating a pretty garden in your home, making a cake for your childhood friends. Meditating, going for a walk, reading, writing. Observing the sky and not doing anything else. The idea is to begin to turn the ordinary into the extraordinary. The world of small things can be very big if you decide that it will be that way. Value and enjoy all that is small. Ideals only exist in your mind, but the small things are the bricks of reality. Mother Teresa of Calcutta said that her mission was "to do all the ordinary things extraordinarily well."

Creative purposes transform the day, turning it into a pleasure to live through it. You connect to your inner purpose so that a deeper meaning might impregnate what you do.

6

Creativity in Relationships

In this chapter I look at different kinds of relationships. I begin with the idea that a relationship involves a bridge that joins two aspects which, in appearance, can be opposed or far from each other. These can be:

- *The past with the future,*
- *The now with the eternal,*
- *The feminine with the masculine and*
- *Hell with heaven, among others.*

For good communication we not only need bridges, but also a language that allows us to understand each other. For this, we have to understand the messages we are given through signs, codes, languages and grammar. We will look at this in the subheading 'Language'.

For relationships to be complete they should be global: you begin with yourself, you continue with the other and you connect with God. The relationships that we have also include our relationship with nature, the material, money and time.

The subheadings that you will find in this chapter are:

- *Creativity in relationships*
- *Building bridges*
- *Language*
- *Complete relationships*
- *With oneself*
- *With others*
- *With God*
- *With nature*
- *With matter*

- *With money*
- *With time*

Creativity in relationships

We have to learn to reinvent relationships so that they are complementary, enriching, healthy, creative, transforming, loving and harmonious. The statistics show that, in 2007, marriages lasted 5.7 years. In the face of the crisis and uncertainty we should care for our relationships. And now, more than ever, this should be a priority. **Let us have the conversations about the subjects that matter with the people that matter to us.**

We also have to reinvent organizations and, as a priority, reinvent ourselves. What happens is that, on reinventing, chaos can ensue and, to avoid it, we stay at a standstill instead of moving forward.

Building bridges

We need creativity to build bridges that join hearts and minds. Bridges shorten distances and allow for communication and getting closer.

Creativity also helps us to build bridges between apparently opposed aspects, to allow us to go from one space to another.

For example, we can connect:

- The present Time, this instant, to Eternity. This allows us to be here in the present and, at the same time, to know that everything is relative. When we connect to eternity, our vision broadens and transcends the trivial.
- The Past to the Future.
- The Past to the Present.
- The Present to the Future.

Time is relative. What exists is the NOW. However, in the stores of our memory we keep archives of past experiences and, every time they emerge onto the screen of our mind, they become present, since they evoke the same feelings that we felt in the past. Also, with our mind, we invoke the future by creating worries, expectations, planning, even fleeing from the present, visualizing a better future, a future salvation.

There is a concept of time that I learned in India and that I want to share here: *trikaldarshi*. To be *trikaldarshi* is to be the one who sees and is conscious of the three aspects of time: past, present and future.

- Past: you see your remote past, the original past, your origin, your naked self, clean of influences, without addictions, unpolluted. It is your divine origin.
- Present: you see your being now, with its stains and its potential, with its weaknesses and its strengths.
- Future: you see Vishnu (see page 92), you see your complete being as the goal that you can come to achieve to live in its full form.

To be *trikaldarshi* also helps you to:

- Past: see your errors; see where you slipped up.
- Present: not to trip over the same stone again. Discern and decide so as to not create opposite reactions to what you want in the future. You know that if you say or do a certain something the other will react badly and this is not what you want.
- Future: your dream made reality.

Other bridges that we can build are those that connect:

The old to the new:
- This connection allows us to see the power and the beauty of the new and makes it easy for us to let go of the old and

let it die.

- Saint Paul says: "You were taught with reference to your former way of life to lay aside the old man who is being corrupted in accordance with deceitful desires, to be renewed in the spirit of your mind, and to put on the new man who has been created in God's image – in righteousness and holiness that comes from truth" (Ephesians 4:22-24).

• The Masculine to the Feminine (the eternal masculine and the eternal feminine). This allows us to manage to complete our being, developing all the qualities.

• Hell with Heaven. Seeing the contrasts allows us to discern and decide where to direct our attention and focus our creative energy. On what level of consciousness do we want to live?

Language
The creative inner language is made up of all the words, images, smells, sounds or other symbols that have any meaning for you. It is not only about knowing how to read the signs, but of also knowing how to understand them.

We have:

• The signs.
• The grammar.
• The languages.
• The codes.

Often we understand neither the signs nor the messages that these codes, signs and languages are trying to communicate to us. We don't understand them and each other because the noise level is high. We need silence to listen and understand. Mutual understanding and comprehension require a subtlety that transcends the codes.

A clear language that does not give rise to misunderstandings or confusion arises out of HONESTY: of the sincerity in what you want to say and in listening objectively.

There are people who communicate with animals. Learning to see, listen to and read the 'unconventional' signs and codes is an art of creativity. To do it you have to be awake, in harmony and use your intuition.

The Australian aborigines communicate with nature. Most of us as westerners have lost this capacity, as we don't respect it as an entity with its own rights; we don't understand its power.

When our mind is in silence we can listen to and understand the signals. The signals that we are given by:

- Time.
- Nature.
- Animals.
- The body.
- The other.
- God.

In the same way that a lighthouse gives off signals and the captain of the ship has to understand them, we receive multiple signals and, as captains of our life, we should learn to decipher them and understand them if we want to travel well and not crash into the cliffs.

With a calm mind and serene heart we know how to pick up and understand the signals that situations are giving us and we also pick up on the signals of time, the moment we are living in. What is more, we are able to understand people, given that we observe, listen to and feel all the languages they are communicating with: the look, gesture, position, vibration, intention, feeling and word.

We often go so fast that, when we speak to each other, we do it in a routine and boring way, without a spark. We are not creative communicators. Let's return to what is basic which is being in the present. When you are opposite someone but your mind is in the past or the future, on what you have to do next or what happened before, then you are not present and the communication with that person is really laborious; you neither listen nor speak out of the power of presence. You lose the opportunity for an optimum encounter and it remains a common, ordinary encounter, with nothing new or special.

Let us use creativity to create a different communication. Go to what is essential. Communicate through generating experiences. Speaking transforming words, that heal, that elevate and connect hearts.

Dialogue can lead us to transformation. With the power of words, a clear intention and the purpose of improvement, let us have conversations that generate positive changes. **Let us bring about the conversations that we have never had. We can create the world that we want.**

Complete relationships

Complete relationships are holistic. They are inclusive, not excluding. Not only the relationship of you and I, but more than you and I. We don't suffocate each other; rather we grow and broaden our horizons. We do not belong exclusively to one another. We are not suffocated in the relationship; rather we flourish and offer the sum of our presence and strengths to the world. The power and energy of talent and essence, when they complement each other, multiply.

Let us see some relationships in which we have to be creative to create, sustain, reinvent and grow:

- With oneself.
- With others.
- With God.
- With nature.

- With the material.
- With money.
- With time.

With oneself

Wherever you go, you go with yourself. If you are fine with yourself, it will be easier to be fine in your surroundings and with others. If you are comfortable with yourself, you will not flee from either yourself or solitude. You will delight in being alone and being with others.

Have creativity to create and improve the relationship between the feminine and masculine in you. Sometimes we spend time wishing that 'another' could satisfy and fill the space of deficiency that we feel. But you will fill this emptiness when you REconnect to your true essence. REmember the power of the RE that I wrote of in the previous chapter.

Having a good relationship with yourself means relating to your being, in harmony with your mind, your emotions, your spirit and your body. If you don't sustain a good emotional relationship with yourself, then you will abuse your body by generating addictions.

Sometimes we are not kind to our mind. We force it and generate a forest of thorns of chaotic thoughts instead of a garden of fragrant, beautiful and colorful flowers.

We pressurize the mind with the desires we have: I want this or I want to be like someone else. You start by liking something, then you desire it and you want it, then you come to need it, then you depend on it until it becomes an addiction. In all the process, your mind has been pressurized.

Self-punishment

We are creative when it comes to punishing ourselves. Let's change the focus and learn to be creative in order to be loving towards ourselves and knowing how to take care of ourselves.

Why do we punish ourselves?

- We don't feel that we deserve something: I don't have the right to...
- If others see that you treat yourself like that, they will treat you like that too. How will they value you if you don't value yourself?
- You fail, you fall, you make mistakes and you feel that you are not worthy.
- You take your mistakes too much to heart.
- You see yourself according to how others see you and, if you don't fulfill their expectations, you punish yourself for it.

Let's be honest: sometimes we prefer to feel guilty than to change. The guilt in which we don't take on the responsibility to change leads us to punish ourselves. We prefer to blame ourselves rather than change a pattern of behavior. With that attitude, we feel heavy, not light. We find it difficult to flow and adapt. We are rigid.

The relationship with others

We think that we are awake, but in reality we are asleep and not aware of it. We live more in the image than in reality. We have built a personality that annuls our essence, and, in the end, we no longer know who we are.

How can you relate to others if not from your awareness? Is it possible to truly meet the other in this way?

Where are we, and how close are we to the other when we are not capable of seeing them consciously, not even of seeing ourselves? Truly meeting the other is to have a relationship in which there is closeness, even though physical distance might separate us.

To create this closeness we need to be able to understand the other, understand that he or she also has their traumas, has possibly turned away from their essence, has allowed themselves to go along with internal and external factors that have distanced them from being themselves. Having compassion and accepting the other are necessary values in order to create a good relationship.

Daring

To dare to build bridges in order to get close is fundamental to creating a healthy relationship where communication can flow. That daring helps us to come out of the silence, fear and cowardice. That way we can build healthy relationships.

In relationship to others, I dare with courage to live in an awakened form, to see, to be attentive, to take an interest in the other, to go into their matters in depth, to put myself in their shoes, to understand them, to open my eyes in order to see.

I dare to break down barriers, defenses, to knock down walls, to break structures in order to reach the deepest part of myself, what I really am.

Helping each other

Often we want to help the other. We are tempted to solve the other's problem. Until we understand that nobody needs to be saved from their path, we will not be able to help each other mutually. Rather, instead of helping each other, it is better to accompany one another in our processes of change. Each one has their lessons to learn and each one has to save themselves. When someone offers you help it is easy to get attached to him or her and believe that they will save you from your difficulties. But nobody can save you. You have to make the move.

If you want to bring light to someone's path, increase your own light.

Often it is enough to be present and listen to the other if the other needs it, but don't do anything, don't start giving advice.

Accompany them with your presence, your silence and your embrace. That way you will act as a mirror for them to see themselves. The solution is within them. What has to transform, improve or be applied in their life, they will do when their time comes. Don't force it.

Remember that, according to Freud, what most bothers us about others is in reality a hidden reflection of ourselves. It is the projection onto others of aspects that bother us about our personality, but that we do not consciously recognize as ours. In these cases, helping the other is a way of escaping from those aspects of our own.

On occasion we cannot bear to see someone else suffer, and we want to prevent them from having this suffering. Suffering at times is necessary in order to cleanse oneself, to recognize, to want to change and transform oneself. We do not know the deep reasons for the other's suffering.

Once an experiment was carried out with butterflies. To come out of the cocoon, they have to make an enormous effort; it almost seems as if they feel pain and suffer in order to make a hole in the cocoon. So, a researcher cut the cocoon very carefully to help the butterfly come out of the cocoon without suffering. Time and again, the butterflies that had been helped to come out using this method died.

The discovery was that the butterfly, in the effort that it makes to come out of the cocoon, moves the liquids of its body towards the wings, which strengthens them, gives them vitality and thus it will be able to use them and fly. But if we help it to come out without effort it dies, since it remains an invalid. We have to be careful that, in helping someone not to suffer, we don't make them into an invalid.

Creativity to generate happiness

Laughing is very healthy. In laughing we stimulate the production of endorphins, the so-called happiness hormones.

They are the natural painkiller, given that they act on the nervous system to reduce sensitivity to pain and make us feel good. If you want to help others creatively, generate happiness and spaces of laughing and cheerfulness. That way you will reduce others' tensions. Laughter is like an inner relaxing massage.

Leading others to a space of happiness and gratitude generates healthy relationships. It helps us to see reality from another perspective, it gives us a broader vision and it helps us to see the benefits and the lessons; it helps us to confront, to let go, to be ourselves without negative influences, without shadows.

The relationship with God

To know someone and relate to them, you devote time to them and you generate spaces to share. It is the same thing in relation to God. People will come in and out of your life. But God is always there. You should develop the relationship and devote time to it if you want to feel it.

It is a relationship that has to be based on a mature understanding, not on desperation, nor on asking and pleading. People ask of God out of desperation, to the point that this becomes a social ritual.

It is a relationship based on friendship. You put yourself on the level of your divinity, your light and you can look into the eyes of God (metaphorically) without feeling guilty or humiliated. Don't lose sight of God by looking at the floor. God loves you as you are, you don't need to be a perfectionist so that He might love you more.

In a mature relationship where there is integration, you integrate with the other, whether the other is a person or God. There is not a mistaken kind of respect in which you feel that God is everything and you are nothing. That is a false act of praise. It is, in fact, a lack of respect. It is true that in God you find the Universe and, therefore, the feeling of the Whole. In communion with Him you feel whole and full.

It is not a parasitic relationship that sucks out your energy until you are weak and exhausted. Here lies the greatness of this relationship: it always gives you energy, love and strength.

You need creativity to integrate God into your life. You decide if you want to carry on living ignoring Him or leaving Him to one side because 'He is of no use to you'. Don't treat Him like an old coat kept in the cupboard that even in winter you don't remember that you have.

How do I integrate God into my life?

In the mornings, in the silence, I open myself to Him and I listen. Not hurrying. Not forcing.

I write Him poems; I tell Him that I love Him. I feel Him.

I find moments of silence during the day and I stop, I look at God and He is there, looking at me. He embraces me. Then I realize that everything is relative, everything changes and that life is a dance, it stops being a battle and an obstacle race.

At night I hand over to Him my accumulated baggage, He dissolves it and then I go with Him and the angels accompany me in my dreams.

The relationship with nature
Don't stop marveling at its existence, its greatness, its silence, its melody.

Give thanks that the plants give you fruit, fragrance and nutrition. The trees, oxygen, fruit and shade. The sun illuminates you. The moon reminds you that everything is cyclical. On the night firmament, the stars remind you that everything is relative, that no problem is as big as it seems. It is the world of the Little Prince. Remember your dreams.

Appreciate nature, let it marvel you and respect it.

Don't misuse it, don't abuse it, pollute it or dirty it.

In old times agriculture was based on a deep respect for

nature. Now, because of greed, the natural cycles have been modified on creating genetically modified seeds. When they are planted, they don't create fertile seeds or feed the nutrients of the earth, so that the earth is impoverished and the agricultural workers too.

Observe how the most creative force is nature: it is creative. More than that of the human being, which is a creating and creative force that has been used and continues to be used in a destructive manner. The maintenance of life is thanks to nature. It sustains, it gives life, it revitalizes and generates itself. To do so it follows patterns, axioms or universal laws, which I look at in the next chapter, 'Universal creativity'.

The relationship with matter

When we use to excess a facility, an object, a resource, we go to the extreme and end up using it badly and causing scarcity. Then, instead of being a facility, it is a burden or an addiction.

For example, when you no longer communicate with someone through speaking and you only do it via the computer, then you are using the computer badly, you are no longer creative in your communication. You look for what is easy: the facilities that technology offers you, and you lose creativity. You hide behind words and the screen.

When you use facilities to entertain yourself, you are not thinking creatively, they attract you, they distract you and they trap you.

Society has become mechanical, instead of creative. We misuse technology and the facilities it offers us.

We nurture laziness: we go for what is easy and we atrophy our creativity. This is one of the reasons why the systems of the world are breaking down. In general, the world is not creative-creating, but rather mechanical. The consumer society is inter-ested in us living mechanically because this is more predictable. If we respond like machines do, the market, consumption, are more predictable; reactions can be quantified, etc. and that way we can be more controlled by the law of supply and demand. The ego-system is interested in having controllable people who respond according to predictable stimuli.

The relationship with money

Throughout history, the relationship with money has tended to be less and less creating and creative of spaces of positivity. It is clear that I am generalizing and that there are many people with philanthropic attitudes. In olden times, an emperor-king-governor would use part of the wealth to build temples that would be of use to and benefit all the people. It was a creative and constructive use of the wealth.

Today, in the West and in other areas of the world, money is used for power games, to build arms. The statistics are depressing. This is the world created by the ego-system. Possibly you make up a part of the privileged 5% of the worldwide population. It is a privilege but it is also a responsibility. And more so in this time of crisis, in which the banks are falling and the economy seems to be melting down. The crisis is global, not only financial.

Global expenditure, according to the 2006 statistics, indicates to us where our priorities are (taken from the Henley World Study):

Spending in thousands of millions of dollars

Basic education for everyone in the world	6
Cosmetics in the United States	8
Ice creams in Europe	11
Reproductive health of ALL the women in the world	12
Perfumes in Europe and the United States	12
Basic health and nutrition for ALL in the world	13
Food for domestic pets in Europe and the USA	27
Entertainment industry in Japan	45

Cigarettes in Europe	60
Alcoholic beverages in Europe	205
Narcotic drugs	600
Military spending in the world	980

We spend more on cigarettes in Europe than on maternal health in ALL the world. More on cosmetics in ONE COUNTRY (the United States) than on basic education for EVERYBODY. More on domestic pets in Europe and the United Status than on basic health and nutrition in ALL the world.

Here we see the priorities of the ego-system clearly: wealth for a few, pleasures for a few. You possibly belong to that group of the few privileged people. Be grateful for it! Take responsibility!

Money has become the security base for many people: this is not being creative. **Security does not come from money but rather from our intelligence and wisdom**.

Money is a facilitator: it is not an end in itself. It is creative when you use it to benefit what is around you: everybody. Let us use it in the mentality of the eco-system, not the ego-system.

Each action has an impact on your life and on the Universe. It is the law of karma. When you throw away and waste, the return will be that when you are in need, you will not receive. Because of this, learn to use it in a worthwhile and valuable way. And, when you need it, the Universe will provide.

For example, building parks, gardens, temples... to embellish public spaces. To help disabled people. Using part of our salary to benefit others is a creative and constructive way of directing the energy that passes through us to help or accompany our neighbor. Let us use money for our own learning and that of our loved ones, to improve schools, universities and to create new spaces of learning.

Relationship with time

The relationship with time requires creativity and flexibility. For many, this relationship is a source of pain (past), stress (present) and worries (future).

I have dealt with our relationship with time at the beginning of this chapter, under the subheading 'Building bridges'.

7

Universal Creativity

In this chapter we will see how universal creativity lasts over time, transcends cultures and religions, and continues to be valid because it respects the universal principles and laws.

The subheadings of this chapter are:

- *Universal creativity*
- *Creativity and its principles*
- *The power of the full stop*
- *Some universal axioms:*
    *Respect for all things and all live beings.
    *Non-violence.
    *Harmony.
    *Biorhythms and lifestyle.
    *Complementarity.
    *Expansion-essence.

Universal creativity

Universal creativity is inclusive. It is not elitist. Anyone with a minimum capacity for language and abstraction can understand it.

We have a legacy of universal creativity of centuries, even millenniums, ago. For example, the Tao. Even if you are not Chinese, and were not alive two thousand years ago, you can understand it. The Tao offers new ideas that, what is more, are transforming. The Tao is creative and inclusive.

The same can be applied to the teachings of Christ. They are not only comprehensible for (and applicable to) Christians. The 'love one's neighbor as yourself' is a universal message that encourages us to use our creativity to apply it and live it out.

The teachings of Buddha about desires and the suffering they cause are universal.

In *The Cloud of Unknowing*, the fourteenth century book by an unknown monk, we find some universal truths that are still true today:

- Ignorance is the cause of complaints.
- Even when the soul has been washed of its sins and the pain they carry, even then there is no perfect rest in this life.
- The one who doesn't know the powers of the soul nor how they work will be easily deceived and/or will feel let down. The powers identified in this context are: the memory, reason, the will, the imagination and sensuality.
- The apprentice of contemplation should devote himself or herself to three things: reading, thinking and praying.

Universal creativity:

- Is simple.
- Is accessible. People can find harmony with its color, its form, its word.
- Is comprehensible.

Universal is that it is not so abstract that people cannot understand it.

Universal is that it is not so ahead of its time that others do not understand it either in its own time or afterwards. The great ideas that only some understand are not universal. Perhaps the idea is universal but the way of transmitting it is limited and elitist. The message that is ahead of its time can be transmitted in a comprehensible form.

Universal creativity helps us to explore the truth that we are never disconnected from the whole. Like a wave, which is an individual expression but, nevertheless, is never disconnected from the ocean. Feeling ourselves to be joined to the whole produces an acceptance of our circumstances. That way, we stop controlling and have a greater degree of detachment. This union shows our willingness to change, liberate, let go and release.

We have other examples of 'conscious waves' connected to the ocean. Saint Francis of Assisi gave an accessible and universal message that reaches the academy or the intellectual, and the farm worker or the baker. His message touches and pleases everyone. For example:

- I am an instrument of peace.
- I should understand rather than seek to be understood.
- Love nature and make friends with animals.

His relationship with God was real and attractive. His love for God was not institutional, but personal. It was a universal love which he transmitted to others, to nature, and to animals.

Those people with a universal creativity rise above systems without being violent towards them; they rise above systems but they work in the system without being trapped in their limitations. Their universal creativity helps them to see beyond the horizon of the walls that might have impeded them.

We have other examples of universal creativity in different areas of human activity. Einstein, in science; Gandhi, in politics; and Maria Montessori, in education, to only mention a few.

Mahatma Gandhi did not want to use violence to free India. His creativity was universal and he transmitted messages that are powerful and comprehensible for any person. For example: 'Be the change that you want to see in the world'.

Maria Montessori was a doctor. She took care of the poor in the shanty towns of Rome. She was the first woman doctor in Italy. Many were against her. She challenged the system but she did not cause a war. She realized that an educational change was necessary in order for the poor to change their condition. She created some universal principles of learning in education that have been used in many schools in the world.

In any case it is not necessary to be a great scientist, politician, educator, mystic, saint or hero to have universal creativity. My grandfather, Javier Vilanova, used to say that **one should never accept blackmail, because if you do you lose your freedom**. It is a universal message that also requires creative skills to apply it in one's own life.

Mercedes, my mother, explains in her memoirs a clear message of universal creativity that she learned from Xicu, a fisherman from a village of the Costa Brava, barber and a militant idealist, anarchist. She explains an occasion when she went out to fish with him thus: "I disappeared behind the rocks and, on my return, they ask me with fear if by chance I had gone through a tunnel. I affirm that I have always dived in the open sky, when it was not possible to be trapped. Xicu trusts that I will do it well and be prudent but he states: 'For me, the only thing that I am afraid of is the ambition for the fish.' This message strengthens because it leaves aside the useless; I have always remembered this piece of advice which helps me to value my limitations as good decisions in living."

Xicu, like Tchouang-Tseu a long time before him, had understood that a being who primes himself to hunt another forgets the dangers that lie in wait for him and, sooner or later, **he falls into the trap laid for him by his own ambition**. "That is why he was afraid when I was fishing," Mercedes tells us. Like that Chinese hunter, I had my sights set on the murky water and I believed it was clear water. And Xicu, like the Chinese philosopher, surprised by the fragility of the human consciousness which so easily forgets dangers and doesn't know where it is, was asking himself what sense it made to risk one's life in a world of intrigues and violence where some beings always hunt others. To that fisherman it seemed that all calculations are in vain, because our consciousness, which gives us an illusion of mastery, encloses us in this illusion as in a bubble and blinds us. That is perhaps the trap: forgetting that we do not know.

Another testimony to universal creativity is that of a fisherman who was in a Nazi concentration camp and survived. On asking him what it was that kept him alive, he said that it was having been a fisherman, because he had always looked at the horizon. Being in that situation, in infrahuman conditions, he always looked at the horizon, beyond the walls that closed him in. This really is creativity. Let us look at the horizon and leave small-mindedness behind.

Creativity and its principles

If we want our creativity to be universal and at the same time the creator of a new world, let us learn to know the universal laws, to respect them and to follow them. We cannot twist them according to our old way of thinking. If we disobey them, the change is temporary or inexistent. When we break the laws, we lose power in the day to day. Our creativity stops being universal.

We break the law, for example, when we allow another person to interfere with, control or manipulate our lives against our will. Or when we interfere with, control or manipulate the life of another person or their circumstances, against their will — and they allow it —, robbing them of their power, leaving them without power to be who and what they want to be and do.

If we break the will of a person, we rob them of one of the most valuable gifts that they have. It is as if we took their integrity from them.

If you feel that someone has robbed you or has reduced your power and will, reclaim them! Not from that person, but from within you. Bring them out.

The power of the point

The point of power is always in the present moment. It is a law.

Metaphorically, the point can be a seed or a drop.

In nature, the seed contains all the information it needs to be a tree; its nature is to grow at a constant rhythm, go to expansion and return to the seed. The good gardener knows the laws. He knows how the seed works and how, where and when it germinates best. In what earth, with which nutrients, how much water, sun and shade it needs. How to get rid of the weeds. He maintains the space and respects time so that the seed can grow at its own rhythm.

In life we go from the essence to expansion, and from expansion to the essence. We go from the point to the ocean and from the ocean to the point. From the drop to the sea and from the sea to the drop. A drop of water can take on different forms, colors, textures, tastes, fragrances. It can form part of a cloud, a river, the dew, an ocean, the rain. But that drop of water forms part of the existence of the Universe. Sometimes the drop advances quickly, other times it stops on a leaf in the dew of the daybreak, others it turns into a flake of snow. Thus is life: we go from being a drop to form the ocean and from the ocean to being a drop. As a drop — water in essence — we take on different forms, spaces, colors, roles, but our essence is the same.

There is a beautiful Indian legend, told to us by Swami Amar Jyoti, in which a drop turns into a pearl:

Receive the Truth, keep your mind on It, and go into silence. Be like an oyster, which takes the drop of rain water, closes its shell, and dives to the bottom of the ocean. There the drop becomes a pearl.

Penetrate through your subconscious mind to the depth of your being, and your Spirit will shine.

A point is extremely subtle and everything is submerged in it like in a seed. The power of packing, of reducing the expansion to the essence increases the concentration. Then you need less time to create something; you use fewer words to communicate the same thing and you do it better.

When your creativity is associated with universal axioms, you do not break certain laws. You align with them. You integrate without being submissive.

Some universal axioms:
- Respect for all things and all live beings.
- Non-violence.
- Harmony.
- Biorhythms and lifestyle.
- Complementarity.
- Expansion-essence.
- Birth-growth-aging-death-birth.
- New-old-new: the world has got old; it has to renew itself.
- Responsibility. Each one is responsible for their state.

The natural patterns are cyclical, they follow an order, they have symmetry and maintain harmony and life.

Respect for All Things and Live Beings
Imbalance is the result of losing respect, and this brings illness with it.

For example:

- When you do not respect your lungs and you smoke. You are a living chimney. You maintain your brain addiction to nicotine and to other chemical substances that stimulate your neurons. You are addicted to this stimulant.
- You eat wrongly, you do not respect your body and it gets ill.
- You don't put the right thoughts in your mind and you get

stressed.

• When you somatize your problems, the body gets tense and finally ill.

Respecting the body is to sleep well. To eat appropriately. To maintain balance in your life. To be honest with yourself, clarify and unblock in order not to somatize.

A consciousness and attitude that increases respect is when you consider yourself to be a guest in this world. Then nothing is yours, you belong to the whole but you don't possess anything: that way you are detached, you respect everything, you don't force, you don't attack, you consider nature to be sacred. From this consciousness you are present. You don't even consider your body to be yours. It is the temple in which you, the light, you, the consciousness, inhabit. In the awareness of living in a temple you respect it and take care of it as a sacred space.

Out of self-respect and respect towards others you do not allow yourself to be influenced by what does not benefit you or others. You do not fall into submission.

Hippocrates said that the reason for illness is that the balance has been lost because there is no respect. According to him, health is the state of perfect harmony of forces in their balance. People get ill because they do not follow the universal laws, they do not respect the axioms.

Non-Violence
See Non-violent space: Ahimsa, page 117.

Harmony
Each one has their turn in their own time, and sustains a generating rhythm of life. For example, the tree breathes: it inhales and exhales. It generates harmony and respects its rhythms. As human beings we have interfered in the rhythms and in the harmony of nature and our body. We have broken this principle.

Biorhythms and Lifestyle

The body has an internal music with which we can and should harmonize. Any life follows guidelines regulated from within, a mechanism that is similar in men, animals and plants.

The bodily biorhythms are our link to the great rhythms of nature. Living in harmony with the rhythms of the body defeats entropy, something that permits the flow of biological information without restrictions. Living in opposition to the rhythms of the body produces an increase of the entropy that leads us to disorder, unhappiness and illness.

Dr. Daniel Bonet explains that we can live each day as if it is a life. In the morning we are like children that grow with the sun, going on to the youth of spring, the plenitude of the summer, the maturity of the autumn and arriving at the winter of old age. And like that one day after another. Each day has rhythm. Each rhythm is similar but it is renewed.

That is why we normally feel more active and full of physical energy during the first half of the day and more inward-looking the second half. If we follow the natural rhythms of the day, we use less energy and everything develops more easily. Chronobiology (the biology of time) studies the effects of these cycles on daily life, and researches into, among others, the circadian rhythm —the day and the night— of the different bodily functions. In this way we know, for example, when it is best to eat certain kinds of food.

It is good for you to listen to your body in order to understand your vital cycles and respect the biorhythms. For example, having dinner very late, and eating a lot, is harmful to the biorhythm. It does not make it easy to rest well and this has an influence on the bodily and emotional state the next day.

People who work on night shifts never manage to get used to the inversion of the vital cycle of being awake and sleeping. The body finds it difficult to adapt to rhythms that disrupt its natural biorhythm. People who work on airlines and are constantly going through time zone changes, confuse their bodies, they don't know when it is time to have lunch or dinner or sleep. On breaking their biorhythms, they lose vitality and health.

Out of work obligations perhaps someone has to break their biorhythmic cycle. In any case, whenever possible, it is good not to voluntarily break it, thus creating damaging habits for one's bodily, mental and emotional health.

It is good to go to sleep early and to wake up early, with the dawn, and thus take in all the energy of the dawning sun, begin with the silence of the dawn, meditating and breathing in the creativity that bursts through the morning calm.

As I have been writing this book, various people have asked me: "How do you manage to be so creative when writing? We try it, but there are so many interruptions. The time just goes." One of the secrets is this: respect the biorhythms: go to bed early and wake up before the dawn so that, when the sun comes up, one is ready to create and write.

Complementarity

Complementarity is the natural law that helps us to co-operate. In nature and in the kingdom of plants and animals, it operates constantly. On complementing us, the synergy comes which leads us to true co-operation.

People don't realize the power of complementarity because of their individualism. They want to be the first. They have the ambition of power, of being someone, of standing out. It is also good to be second and not always be the first. When we complement each other the best of each person emerges and we bring together strengths, talents and energy.

On competing, you aren't aware of what you can offer. You lack perception, and you don't know how to complement. On not knowing and not perceiving it correctly, a lack of respect occurs. Without respect, it is not possible to complement each other.

A person who is disturbed, unstable and that is facing

downwards, like a bat, does not know themselves, does not respect themselves and does not have the power to complement. They compete and, then, a great waste of energy is caused.

Complementing is more than the harmony of the Yin and Yang. We could say that complementing each other is to be like the five fingers on a hand, which are different but complement one another and work together. The two legs, the arms and the eyes complement each other. As people we can complement each other in a task and, together, out of complementarity, we can move mountains. As there is not conflict or competitiveness, we save a lot of energy and we channel it where it is necessary. With less, we achieve more.

Expansion-Essence

One of the characteristics of the Universe is that it expands and it contracts. The Universe functions in cycles which go from the essence to expansion and from expansion to the essence. In nature, we see for example how the seed becomes a tree and the tree becomes a seed. The seed grows and expresses, and then it returns to being a seed to express itself again.

The signs of expansion are:

- The infinite.
- The enormous.
- Extroversion.
- Chaos.
- Entropy.

Now we are in a period when expansion has reached an extreme.

The moment has arrived to return to the essence. This is the moment of change, which can take place any instant.

When you go from expansion to the essence, you let go of the layers of the soul and connect with the silence of your being. The body and your being change on accepting and incorporating your new identity. This can happen from one moment to another. The next instant anything can happen. Change can be rapid when you let go.

To go to the essence

Melt down the expansion, like the spider eats the web. In our case, it means going to silence. Thinking and talking less. Refining your feelings. Spending less time on something. Being more centered.

Going to the essence gives better results, greater experience and more success. You love more and better.

Going to the essence is to go to the unity of concentrated energy. The infinitesimal characterizes the essence. The atom. When you divide it, you generate the expansion of atomic energy.

Invisible reality, the basic and essential unity, is the atom. In the spiritual it is the atma, the atmic energy, the energy of your conscious being, of the soul.

In human time, the essential unit is the second. In a second you breathe, in a second you think. **How creative can you be in that second?**

The essence is for example in the power of the patience of a second. The patience that you have for that second before reacting.

A second can be powerful, successful, worthy and valuable. How many seconds do you waste per minute, per hour, in a state of unawareness, of being asleep to life, to reality and to your creation (your thoughts and feelings)? How many seconds get away from you in a state of tension, nervousness, impatience and intolerance?

In a second you accept and harmonize. Some seconds of silence help you to go into sound from the calm and then you express yourself clearly, in a stable, non-aggressive way. That seed of a second expands into something creative that emerges from your being in connection to the other.

The essential unity of mental creation is thought. A thought is the essence. How much power is there in a thought?

For example, think I AM PEACE: you take two or three seconds to think it. How much power is there in those two or three seconds?

You can concentrate with your breathing. It is not a question of technique, but of really feeling it. Think and breathe: "I am a soul of peace." In four seconds you feel it and, to the extent that you repeat it, it forms part of you.

In a second you can feel, listen and transform. But your mind says to you, "Hurry up, you are wasting time," and you, rapidly, start to run again... although you don't know very well where to. Then, curiously, instead of accumulating seconds, you lose them. You go to expansion.

A law connected to the essence and expansion is applied to learning. To learn, you begin with the lowest unit. You learn language first with short words and the simplest verb tense. Then you go to expansion. From expansion you have to return to the seed to remember the essential comprehension.

For example, you learn how the car works, the engine, the lights, the gearshift, the battery, the oils, the tools. Then you return to the essence, to the basics: knowing how to put the keys in, start, use the steering wheel, the gears and the pedals.

Philosophy has distanced itself from the basic unity. Theology has confused more than clarified. Buddha, Christ, Saint Francis of Assisi speak of the basic units; they go to the essential. Their messages are clear, plain and concise.

The *Bhagavad Gita* is 18 chapters, a relatively short book, and yet there are so many interpretations, so many written texts based on it, that they turn into intellectual squandering. So many theological interpretations have complicated and distanced people from spirituality. The people that do not have experiences stay glued to the book and become dogmatic. With so much explanation, so much interpretation, finally we forget the essence and, without the essence, knowledge becomes theoretical, twisted and complicated. This in the end has distanced people from religion and from spirituality.

From expansion to the essence and vice versa

In narcissist expansion you feel good, but nobody understands you. With narcissism neither are you collaborating in creating a new world.

People get lost in expansion, they become intellectual and they do not feel.

Expansion is good as long as we return to the experience of the essence. Let us return to the basic, to the essential unity. The natural rhythm is cyclical: essence-expansion-essence-expansion.

Throughout the history of the great religious traditions people appear who take things once again to their essence, while others seem to return to expansion. Some of those who lead things to the essence are:

- Saint John of the Cross.
- Saint Teresa of Ávila.
- Saint Francis of Assisi.
- Master Ekhart.
- Juliana of Norwich, with her book *Revelations of the Divine Love*.
- Hildegard von Binguen, a tenth century German woman, who expounded advanced ideas, she was a healer, she wrote music and was a mystic.
- The anonymous English monk, with his text *The Cloud of Unknowing*, which I wrote about at the beginning of this chapter.

In other religious traditions we also find people who take the Koran, the Gita or other religious messages to their essence, thus connecting them to the universal nature of the message.

8

Spiritual Creativity

Spiritual creativity helps us to live in wholeness. This chapter begins with understanding that the spiritual is practical. We start by seeing how spiritual creativity helps us in illness. We will see the symbol of personal sovereignty in Vishnu, which balances the feminine and the masculine. His ornaments give us the key to having an open state of awakened consciousness, the practical method to maintain our inner power, its application in our personal life and the mission that fills each one of our acts with meaning.

We will learn from the tortoise that retires within itself and comes out according to its need.

Spiritual creativity helps us to be contemplative in action.

We will see how spiritual creativity connects us with awakening, salvation and illumination.

To finish the chapter, I write briefly about spirituality in art.

The subheadings in this chapter are:

- *Spiritual creativity*
- *Spiritual creativity in illness*
- *Nourishing oneself with Vishnu*
- *The tortoise: creativity to go inwards and outwards*
- *Karma yoga*
- *In the silence*
- *Creativity to awaken*
- *Spirituality in art*

Spiritual creativity

To be spiritually creative is to know how to live. Using spiritual creativity helps you to be in constant transformation and, as a result, you live in freedom. You don't cling to anything. You are agile like the light. The moment comes in which you realize that, in fact, you don't have to transform anything, change is an illusion, you only have to let go of your baggage, your defenses and the mirages in order to be what you are in your essence.

Our level of spirituality doesn't have to do with what we believe but rather with everything that we do with our state of consciousness. That determines how we act in the world and how we interact with others.

Christ taught us to live in this spiritual creativity, out of the love and compassion that arises out of the inner space, of the connected being, 're-linked'.

There have also been artists who have connected to this essence. For example, Kandinsky was interested to find and emphasize in his works the point of spiritual contact; this point of contact referred to the intention of the 'pure artists' to transmit the essential through their artistic creation. Eastern art was also dedicated to this search and called it contact with the 'originary force', with the 'absolute truth', with the principle from which we all, as beings, arise.

Spiritual creativity:

- Is to go beyond divisive dogmas, so that there can be unity in diversity.
- Is to have empathy.
- Is to know how to forgive when there are conflicts.
- Is to live humility in power.
- Is to apply values in technology.
- Is to live service in leadership, be a serving leader, not an ego-led leader.

Spiritual creativity is necessary in order to build a global village, a new world.

Spiritual creativity in illness

Spiritual creativity helps us in illness. When illness comes, it is accompanied and even supported by weakening attitudes that have blocked our energy.

What virtue and attitude is the necessary medicine to heal the soul and help the body?

The first thing is to have the courage to look inside and stop escaping from yourself. On opening the inner 'cupboard', you will see that many feelings are stored there. Buried live feelings never die and they end up by gestating illnesses and pains, Karol K. Truman states.

When you are conscious of the feelings that you store inside, perhaps you will be scared, you feel insecure or impotent. It is there that spiritual creativity is useful. Focus on the virtue that you have to use and the attitude that you should take. For example, it might be:

- The virtue of loving yourself and an attitude of forgiving yourself.
- The virtue of silence and an attitude of acceptance.
- The virtue of courage and a decisive attitude.
- The virtue of clarity and an attitude of trust.

When you stop being in denial and accept that you have these accumulated feelings, the power will emerge in you to confront them. That way you will be able to let them go. The inner space will stay clean so that healing energy and the life force can flow. Hippocrates said that illness is due to the imbalance between the humors and the life force.

For Hippocrates, known as the father of Medicine, health is the state of perfect harmony of forces in balance. Illness has the task of re-establishing the disturbed balance; therefore, it is a reaction of conservation. Health and illness are the two functions that have the same objective: the conservation of life. Aware that health is the most valuable patrimony that the human being possesses, Hippocrates threw out the well-known aphorism that prescribes: "Let your food be your medicine, and your medicine your food."

Nourishing oneself with Vishnu

Spiritual creativity nourishes and sustains. One of the most complete symbols of personal mastery and sustenance of the self is Vishnu, an Eastern divinity. To nourish the self means that there are no deficiencies, and to sustain it means that the elevated level of creation is maintained; it doesn't decay, it doesn't go into the entropy of waste and routine.

In Vishnu, the feminine integrates with the masculine, which does not depend on the gender of the person. Each one of us, man or woman, can be Vishnu. The masculine creates in taking initiative and leads it. The feminine nourishes it and sustains it.

Ekhart Tolle reminds us that, in the ancient pre-Christian civilizations such as the Sumerian, the Egyptian and the Celtic, they respected and even venerated the feminine principle. Then, throughout history, it seems that the feminine sacredness has been suppressed. Tolle tells us that the suppression of the feminine principle, especially in the last two thousand years, has allowed the ego to take on an absolute supremacy over the collective human psyche. In the present day, the suppression of the feminine has been interiorized by many women. As feminine sacredness is suppressed, many women perceive it as an emotional pain.

The intuition is usually more present where the feminine principle is strong, probably because the feminine tends towards opening and the sensitivity to nourish and care for others. The barriers and fears favored by the more competitive masculine conditioning tend to deny the skill of perceiving the subtle energies both in formal and informal relationships.

Vishnu is related to consciousness and attitude, not to the

gender of the person, be they woman or man. Vishnu does not create and let go of what is created, but rather nourishes it until it is grown and self-sufficient. It sustains it and then lets it go so that it can have life of its own. It is the art of creating, sustaining and letting go.

It teaches us not to be possessive with our creation. This also applies to oneself. If in a given moment you manage to create a state of well-being and enjoyment, and then you attach yourself to that state, the fear arises in you of losing it. Out of attachment and fear you lose it, because clinging on creates stagnation. Being Vishnu means knowing how to sustain your state of enjoyment and wholeness through living in *this* moment and not the memory of that moment in which you felt the enjoyment.

The difficulty that we have in this world created by the ego-system is that, when you sustain your creation, you attach yourself to it, you depend on it and then you don't let it grow, and what you have created dies due to asphyxiation.

To sustain is to nourish until the creation can maintain itself.

Vishnu has four arms which indicate this integration of the feminine and the masculine in the person.

Each hand has an object which symbolizes:

- The discus: the state of consciousness.
- The mace: the method.
- The lotus flower: application in one's personal life.
- The conch shell: the mission.

The discus of self-realization

It symbolizes the state of consciousness. What discus plays in your mind and your heart? What is the song that repeats itself? That the discus of self-realization plays in your mind and your heart means that:

- **You are** aware of who you are.

- **You think** ideas that arise from your being and not from the superficiality of the external.
- **You feel** personal eternity: you are always. You do not die because your body ends. You are not the body. You neither end, nor finish because your possession ends. You are not the possession. You do not end because your role as a manager or your role as a mother ends. You are not the role.
- **You live** continuity, the cycle of life. If a plant continues, it always leaves seeds. Would not a person, a being, also have continuity? Nature has four seasons. We live the day and the night. To live the cycle is to know how to go from one period to another, allowing the old to die and making it easy for the new to be born. It is to respect the biorhythms.
- **You see** your essential and original being.

The mace: self-mastery

It is the symbol of the method that gives you power to be Vishnu. It is to have mastery over your feelings. To lead our attention away from our victim part and to give it to our creative part. Where our attention is placed is where the energy flows and, where the energy flows, this grows and is strengthened.

The lack of mastery would be:

- Being a victim.
- Being a complainer. Complaining is a manifestation of impotence and, in practice, not only does it not work but on the contrary, it is a way of giving strength to the problem and not to the solution.
- Being the one that blames others.
- Comparing. From comparison comes jealousy, envy, constant dissatisfaction.
- Being worried: What fear do you have that makes you worry so much? What do you fear that makes you allow

this assault of worries that invade your creative space and block it?

What is it that you don't master?

- If you complain: you don't have mastery over yourself nor do you accept situations. You have too many expectations and you want the Universe to dance to your music. You lose your happy state and remain in a state of dissatisfaction.
- If you compare: you lack knowledge of yourself. You have a lack of respect towards yourself. Without self-knowledge or self-respect, you look outside for what you have within and you don't find it, because you already have it.

Personal mastery is not to be controlling. Sometimes we confuse mastery with control. The controller wants to keep people and situations under control, something that is practically impossible. The controller is not a good observer; because of this he does not have the capacity to participate. He finds shared life, team work and co-operation difficult.

To participate means to take one step backwards and one step forwards. That is, a step back to observe, to leave space for the other, for him or her to be and to express him or herself. To take a step forward in order to participate and play the game, to be present in and with others. On not being a good observer, the controller does not understand what the most effective way of participating is.

Being a controller indicates that there is an inner insecurity. Although the controller manifests strength, in reality it is hiding personal insecurity. There is a deep ego that believes: I know better, I know more.

Self-mastery is to have balance. For example, with responsibility. Sometimes you are over-responsible. You try for things to go well and the opposite occurs. If you have an erroneous sense of responsibility you go to the extreme. When this happens, you don't relate adequately to the time, to the situation nor to people. A person who is too responsible thinks that everything depends on them.

The contrary are those who do not take on responsibility: they leave it all to others, they are passive, lazy and careless.

Self-mastery comes out of the power of the RE: Reunite, Re-link and Remember (explained in the chapter, Transformative Creativity.)

The lotus flower

It is the symbol of harmony that arises from the purity of the self: unstained, unpolluted, unadulterated. It is the integrated self, coherent and transparent. It has nothing to hide.

It thinks, feels and says the same. It is aligned. It is *one* with itself, with others, with God and with the whole.

The lotus flower is being and applying the virtues in practical life.

The conch shell

It is the symbol of the mission and the purpose. It is to serve and to give, being a connecting bridge. To give is to give oneself and to give oneself is to live fully.

The conch shell shows the generosity of sharing (not only giving, since to give implies to take). That way you go from deficiency to feeling yourself complete and from there to sharing. Relationships flow well when each one feels complete. On completing yourself and being like Vishnu, you discover that you are unique in a non-selfish way.

The result of living out the inner Vishnu, of being conscious and taking the four symbols to your practical life is that you know how to live in harmony. **That is why the essence of spiritual creativity is knowing how to live**.

The tortoise: creativity to go within and outside

It is the creativity to enter into sound and action when you want to and it is necessary, and to remain in silence and introspection when you decide to. The tortoise goes inside its shell or comes out, according to its need. It disconnects its organs from the senses and stays inside, in the tranquility of its being.

When we are propelled into action in an automatic way, we lose creative capacity and act out of habit and habitual reaction. This creativity helps us to brake, to stop, to reflect, to value silence and non-action. Out of the experience of silence we value our energy more and we give more value to each word, each gesture, each action and each expression.

It is creativity that allows you to see what brings meaning. It is creativity that allows you to listen to the essential.

We are surrounded by noise, both outside and within. It is in our hands to quieten the inner noise. We can use our creativity to quieten.

We need creativity so that which is deep can impregnate what you do.

With this art of going a moment into the silence and in the next entering into action you become a channel, an instrument through which the presence, the divine energy and peace enters into this world.

In the silence you create consciousness and you bring it to sound. You don't get lost on going into action. You maintain an elevated consciousness.

Karma yoga

It is the art of keeping the consciousness awake while you are in action. It is to act out of your highest self. It is to be in yoga, in connection, in contemplation, in the power of the RE, while you are in the karma, in the action.

Silence is the base of creativity, because in silence we clarify ideas, we discern, we reconnect to the essence and to the intuition. Our being fills with tranquility and peace.

Braking the impulse towards action and allowing yourself a space of 'non-doing' (although you are always doing, even when you are not doing) is not a waste of time. Many think that silence is passive, that it is the negation of expression and action. I would say, rather, that not being able to stop doing, being in constant movement, planning and action can come to be a flight from oneself, and even a negation of the self. This is why many end up getting ill, since nature is wise and the body obliges us to brake and stop ourselves in order to listen and to see.

In fact, the creativity that arises in the silence guides you in order to show you how to relate and connect. It is the creativity of karma yoga, of silence in action. Of being connected within while you are connected with everything that surrounds you.

In the silence

In the silence you are an observer, not because you have had enough nor to criticize. You have a creative observation. You see meaning in the things that are scattered and disordered. The pieces of the puzzle, of the mosaic, join and harmonize in the silence.

In silence you concentrate. You go beyond the mental chatter. With a powerful thinking that takes you higher you stop producing dozens of thoughts and you save energy. You use this creativity to listen to the signals and perceive the messages through the sound and noise.

The important thing is to reconnect with yourself and, from there, to God and to the world. It is a matter of a second. A second of patience, of peace, of silence, connects you to your intuition. In a second you create a thought that is the seed for many conse-quences. These depend on the quality of the thought, of the seed. In a second you open a space to nourish, grow and learn.

In the silence you are creative and conscious through thought and through feeling. Then you go to expression and action; to the color and sound.

Silence is the bridge that connects us to the realities that exist and function beyond our logic and senses. Silence joins us to the deepest essence of our being, facilitating closeness and connection to the self and the other, whatever the other is... person, sound, light, feeling, color, nature, God.

In the silence we touch the traces of eternity.

Creativity to awaken

A century ago now, in 1911, Kandinsky wrote: "Our soul, which after a long materialist period is still in the beginnings of awakening, contains germs of desperation, of the lack of faith, lack of objective and of meaning."

Awakening is a term that we have used more in this last century, and especially from the end of the decade of 1960 and the beginnings of 1970. However, the religious traditions have spoken to us about it for years, in different terms, such as for example:

- Enlightenment and liberation (Jivan Mukti, Hinduism).
- Salvation (Christianity).
- The end of suffering (Buddhism).

Anthony Strano tells us about illumination that

When the mind is still, silent, detached
then thought becomes a thread that stitches itself to God.
To be combined with God brings a consciousness
beyond matter, time, even thoughts.
This is enlightenment.
Honest communication with God means
to meet Him as I am, how I am.

Depending on how you position yourself to receive, learn and transform, enlightenment will come to you.

This is not a book about salvation nor do I want to enter into great theological discourses. Salvation understood as being and living liberated in life, the Jivan Mukti, consists in freeing yourself from selfish needs. When you are liberated in life you can relate to the other, to time, food, others, connecting to the whole. There is harmony. You do not only save yourself. When you experience liberation in life you are not on your own, isolated; rather you harmonize with nature and the material.

To reach this state you need a creative intellect that can integrate and balance. With the creative intellect you neither analyze nor understand in a conditioned way. You are far from being conditioned. That is recognition, salvation.

The end of suffering is the end of the samsara. The wheel of desire ends. To reach this state you have to see adequately. The creative intellect sees where things are taking you before it is too late. You can put the brake on in time and change the direction.

For this kind of creativity you need humility: to retire from yourself. To detach from yourself. It is an exercise of extraordinary humility and inner will because, on doing it, you feel that your ego dies and resistances of all kinds emerge.

To end the wheel of desire is to cultivate an authentic, not illusory, happiness. Suffering comes because you believe that an illusion is true. Attachment gives you the illusion, the appearance, belonging and security. As it is an illusion, you are afraid and jealous. If it were true, you would not be either afraid or jealous.

In essence, to awaken, illuminate oneself, liberate oneself and save oneself is to be the light of the consciousness. It is not a question of fighting against the ego, in the same way that one does not fight against the darkness. It is only necessary to put on the switch and turn the light on. It is to switch on the consciousness and the light will come on. You are the light.

Saint Paul gives us some guidelines to reach this light:

"Therefore we do not despair, but even if our physical body is wearing away, our inner person is being renewed day by day. For our momentary, light suffering is producing for us an eternal weight of glory far beyond all comparison because we are not looking at what can be seen but at what cannot be seen. For what can be seen is temporary, but what cannot be seen is eternal" (2 Corinthians 4:16-18).

On different occasions, Jesus said to his disciples words that would help them to awaken, to come out of their limitations, to do the contrary to what the routine and custom pushed them to do. For example, he told them: "Therefore I tell you, do not worry about your life, what you will eat, or about your body, what you will wear. For there is more to life than food, and more to the body than clothing." "So do not be overly concerned about what you will eat and what you will drink, and do not worry about such things. For all the nations of the world pursue these things, and your Father knows that you need them. Instead, pursue his kingdom, and these things will be given to you as well. Do not be afraid, little flock, for your Father is well pleased to give you the kingdom" (Luke 12:22-32).

The new world, and the purpose that you have connected to creating it, has to emerge now in you. The change that you want to see in the world you have to live now in you. Not let it be a simple thought about something which will happen, since that would be to wait for a future salvation. Freedom will not be in the future; rather it is now in you. Remember that the power is in your presence now. Only the present can free us. That is to be awake and live with an awakened consciousness.

Spirituality in art

I want to make a brief mention of spiritual creativity in art.

Throughout history many works of art have been created that are related to and inspired by religious, spiritual and/or mystical experiences. From cathedrals to icons, from the sculptures of gods and goddesses, to musical compositions. All these works of art were inspired by transcendent and divine experiences. In general, these works have been realist, representative of figurative art.

Curiously, one of the pioneers in abstract art, Kandinsky, denominates the conceptual and live difference between the spiritual and material world as 'interiority-exteriority'. Through his artistic offerings, he calls to the West to rescue the intrinsic relationship between spirit and the matter.

For Kandinsky, artistic representation is the result of total opening. When the opening reaches its end it is because it has been transformed into spirit; this spirit turns into energy and afterwards, the energy converted into form will give life to the work of art.

9

Art: The Legacy of the Past, the Creation of the Future

In this chapter we will see how art is a legacy of the past and a live witness of something that was and that passed. Art can also be a creation that brings the future forward. This book is not about art, nor only for artists. Creativity is a gift that we all have.

Creativity can be used to repeat the past or to create a new present and future. We will see here how each one of us can be creative in order to bring the future forward for us and live creating a better present.

I will also deal with the importance of taking a leap that challenges the law of entropy and helps us to change our point of departure for good. We will see how to turn our creative capacity into our friend and ally in order to manage to transform ourselves and be what we want.

In this chapter you will find the following sub-headings:

- *The legacy of the past*
- *Creativity to repeat and prolong the past*
- *Creativity to create a new future*
- *Bringing the future forward: preparing oneself in the present*
- *Leapfrog or leap-extraordinaire?*

The legacy of the past

Throughout history we have made multiple attempts to understand the origin of our characteristic creative impulse, approaching through exhaustive research the reason for this creative nature. As human beings, we need to express ourselves, communicate with each other and relate to each other. Art is the legacy left to us by the expression of each civilization, culture and community. The arts transmit the energy, the passion, the beliefs, the systems, the languages, the messages of that civilization, culture or group in particular. They are the plastic expression of the artist or artists that embodied it in their works of art.

We trace the footprints of our history through the artistic legacy of our ancestors, who have been immortalized through their works, architecture, sculpture, writing, poetry, the theatre and music.

Throughout history, artists have often been ahead of their times. Because of this, they haven't been understood by their contemporaries. They have created a new school, breaking with the structure and beliefs of the past and the present, to form a new way of transmitting and expressing their vision of reality and the world.

Spirituality has had a great influence on the history of art. Indeed, both Eastern art and Wassily Kandinsky, Russian painter and musician of the beginning of the twentieth century, converge on attributing spirituality not only the category of being the element from which 'pure art' is born, but also attributing to it the character of fundamental substance that allows for the integral experience between the creator, the piece of work created and the receiver or spectator.

Creativity to repeat and prolong the past

Generally, we create by basing ourselves on concepts and experiences of the past. We are influenced by our past and by the experiences and feelings that we have stored in our personal and collective inner memory. It is as if we lived in a box, that of the past, and were only capable of creating from there. The space, the dimension and what is outside of the box is unknown to us.

In general, we fear the unknown and we cling on to what we know, to what is comfortable, habitual and routine. Any change that means leaving there causes us discomfort, chaos and uncertainty, and that is why we resist change. We prolong what we know: the past.

Creativity to create a new future

We are going to see how to create the future basing ourselves on the vision of **a new woman and man**, free of the burdens of violence, oppression, grief and discrimination of the past and the present. To create the new from the new: coming out of the box of mental limitations. To think outside the limits of the box is to oblige our brain to activate patterns of neuronal connections in a different order and sequence to the habitual ones. While we think and act within the limits of the box we will be limiting our capacity to evolve, progress, or modify our behavior.

Let's use our capacity to create, not to repeat the past, not to demonstrate the present, but to create the future. Not to leave footprints for our descendants of what we have been and of what is happening to us now and what we are, but to create in order to leave our children a better world, a *new* world, without a trace of the old and the destructive.

This means to be capable of creating from another paradigm that is unknown to us, because we haven't experienced it. Nevertheless we can envision and invoke it. It is to create from another level of consciousness that is not trapped by the old schemes of action-reaction, provocation, oppression-oppressed, attack, defense, victim, fear, etc. It is to go forward to the time that we want to arrive at.

Bringing the future forward: preparing oneself in the present

We can bring the future forward, in the same way as the artists have done throughout history. We can create the new that we want to see in the world and live out that change now in our lives. The artists that brought the future forward were not understood in their time. They were labeled mad and nonsensical.

They were marginalized. However, they saw reality from another perspective, and the people of their time that were still living in the old paradigm did not understand them. The future generations were those that were grateful for the courage, the vision and the push forward of those artists of new expressions.

It is to create a personal and collective preparation, not out of fear of what might happen or desperation at what is happening. To create out of fear or out of desperation is to create from the same paradigm in which we live and, therefore, the fruit cannot be something new and different. We would not advance, we would only move energies but we would stay in the same place. This is what often happens. We move many things; in appearance we create, but nothing new or different arises out of that creation. We carry on going round in the same circles.

It is to create as a preparation and anticipation, out of respect for the self, and out of attention and care. Care of the self, of relationships, of the environment and of nature. It is to prepare oneself to have the strength and resources that are necessary to help oneself and co-operate with others.

Leapfrog or leap-extraordinaire?

In sum, it means to create from and out of the new, which means to take a quantum leap. A leap that is not ordinary and that leads to another dimension. A leap that takes you into flight and means that you do not return to the same position. Sometimes we leap but are like the frog that jumps and then falls back in the same position from which it set out.

We have made an attempt to change, but in the end the forces of entropy lead us to the same place or one similar: we return to our chemical, mental and emotional addictions, to our known places. Some of the symptoms that show this are:

- depression,
- anxiety,

- stress,
- apathy,
- the inability to concentrate,
- the difficulty in thinking clearly,
- the desire to continue with the routine of our daily life,
- the impossibility of completing certain actions,
- the lack of new experiences and emotional responses,
- the sensation that one day is the same as another.

We use the people and situations that support us in believing and behaving in accordance with our addiction, for example, to feel like victims. This is only a way of excusing our refusal to change, since, in the end, we determine how we feel, independently of the environment.

Therefore, we have to learn to take an extraordinary leap, beyond the ordinary. It is a leap that sustains itself in the new, that does not return to the old patterns, that does not fall back into addiction, that is not satisfied with the ordinary and that does not make excuses. It does not disintegrate, fade away or break after a short or a long time. It remains in the new, in the essential.

10

The Consciousness Out of Which We Create

We will see in this chapter the importance of the consciousness out of which we create. I will differentiate between two basic consciousnesses: the one that emerges from the ego, from the temporal and hardened self, and the one that emerges from the being, from the essential and authentic identity.

The subheadings in this chapter are:

- *Creating out of the ego character*
- *Creating out of the essential character*

Creativity comes from within. It arises in interaction and in contact with the being of the other. The other can be nature, animals, an object, a space, a piece of work, another person, God.

We create where the space is given for that contact between ourselves and the other. In that contact the creative spark emerges. The self that contacts and from which the creative spark emerges can be:

- *I the ego. It is the ego character that manifests its creativity.*
- *I the soul. It is the essential character that manifests its creativity.*

Both the ego character and the essential being have their roles, ramifications and creative spaces. You can create from your defensive self or from the heart, from the mind or from the intuition, from the familiar habit or from the new unknown.

Let's look at some characteristics of what we create out of the ego-character and what we create out of the essential character.

Creating out of the ego character

From this state of the ego:

- We create problems.
- We generate worry.
- We store up resentments.
- We wait with expectations.
- We have demands.
- We cause anger.
- We feel anxious.
- We resist change.
- We need the praise and approval of others.

The ego feels itself to be lacking and tries to complete itself:

- Through others.
- Through the roles it plays.

We give our power to others. Then we use this 'dis empowerment' by blaming the other as an excuse and as resistance to change. With phrases like 'He made me do it'. 'It was she that decided it'.

The ego demands.

The ego opposes what is.

The ego wastes energy, it crashes; it brings about reactions of resistance.

The ego suffers. From the suffering, one creates creatively. It is an egotistical narcissistic creation. Perhaps therapeutic for the one who creates it. It does not have the power to create a new world because it arises out of a space of egotistical suffering.

From the egotistical state one looks for newness in a narcissistic way. It is superficial. It is not a true newness. We have already looked at this subject in the section 'How new is the new?'

The ego asks: What can I do so that this situation can satisfy my needs, or how can I find another situation which will satisfy me in the future? What is it that will give me what I desire?

The ego lives in the limitation of thought. The limitations arise out of:

- beliefs,
- excuses,
- blaming outside (the other, situations, the dog, God),
- self-concepts,
- fixations,
- complexes,
- taking for granted,
- negation,
- fear, and,
- resistances

The thoughts that come out of these spaces are limiting and do not produce a liberating creation. They leave us where we are or they block us. They even come to create unhealthy situations.

Some examples of thoughts like that are:

- My husband/my wife will not understand me.
- They can't help me with my problem.
- My case is different.
- Nobody else does it.
- They won't let me change.
- They won't understand me.
- I don't want to hurt them.
- Spiritual people don't get angry.
- It is too expensive.
- This would not be spiritual.
- I don't believe it.
- I am not like that.

- I am too old for this.
- I will do it later.
- I am not ready for this.
- Maybe I will fail; I am not up to it.
- They might reject me.
- What will they think?
- Perhaps it will hurt me if I do it.
- I don't want to talk about this.
- There is nothing wrong with me.
- If I ignore it, perhaps the problem will go away.
- I am not good at this.
- If I do it, perhaps my back will hurt.
- I don't have the necessary energy.
- I might lose my freedom.
- It is too difficult.
- It is impossible.

Creating out of the essential character

The truth is that part of our being which does not change; it is eternal, it is our essence. Your true being is your best self. The truth is non-violent. The essence of your true being is non-violent.

When you are in your essence you don't limit yourself to expressing yourself in the way that you want but rather you consider and take the other into account. You are not narcissistic and you can see and feel the other. Out of the essence, you ask what it is that the situation is asking you to do. You respond to the needs of people and situations, not out of submission or the fear of not doing the right thing, but rather out of love and respect. Viktor Frankl reminds us that the important thing is not what we expect from life, but what life expects from us.

When you are centered in your consciousness of being, you act in a way that is appropriate for the whole; you benefit the situation, others and yourself. You are an agent of positivity.

Kandinsky explains: "Little by little we have distanced ourselves from this primordial state; we have developed many false cognates, which have maintained and still maintain today a false idea of union with the essence of existence. We have filled our lives more and more with created needs which are only satisfied by our own creations. It is for this reason that the need for art arises — for creativity — as a point of connection between the real world — already corrupt — and the sensitive world."

Out of the true essence of being, we humanize and create:

- Forgiveness.
- Reconciliation.
- Harmony.
- Understanding.
- Union.
- Trust.
- Patience.

Out of our state of awakened consciousness, we are aware. We are not the dreamer who doesn't know what they dream. Out of this state, **the being knows how to wait, stay open and receive**.

One feels deep and pure emotions. One shares out of that purity of feeling. The awareness of the soul creates positivity. Its creativity is universal and it elevates. It arises out of a genuine and deep space, not from the superficial layers but rather from the essence itself.

The thoughts that arise out of this consciousness are liberating. Let us see some examples:

- I can.
- I dare to.
- I will achieve it.
- I will make myself understood.
- They will support me.

- I trust.
- I will arrive.
- I forgive myself.
- I accept myself.
- I open myself.
- Where I am, everything is fine.
- I let go.
- The resistances don't have power over me.
- I do the best I can.
- Today is wonderful.
- I observe without judging.
- I choose to be free.
- I am power and the world neither suffocates nor annuls me.
- I continue to learn.
- I choose to see myself as the Universe sees me and as God sees me: perfect and complete.
- I am where I have to be.
- The past does not enslave me, it no longer has power over me.
- I can change.
- I begin the clearing of my inner store cupboards.
- I approve of myself.
- I love myself.

Out of the essential character you recognize and live in unison with the whole. There is no separation or conflict. You live in a state of surrender in which you are the bearer of the energy of the origin, the divine energy, for the world.

The new world emerges inside you, in your being, here and now. It is not theoretical. It is a reality when you allow the ego to die and your essential being emerges. In this state you become an instrument, or as Osho said, a flute through which the divine wind blows. Master Hafiz, fourteenth-century Sufi poet, expressed it thus: "I am a hole in a flute that makes the breath of God sing. Listen to his music."

In the Sermon on the Mount, Jesus said:

Blessed are the poor in spirit, for the kingdom of heaven belongs to them (…)
Blessed are the meek, for they will inherit the earth (…)
Blessed are the pure in heart, for they will see God (…).
(Matthew 5:5)

The humble, the dispossessed, the poor, are those that do not have ego, they are those who live awakened in their authentic essential nature. They are the ones who will create and inherit the new world.

11

The Space That Creativity Bursts
Forth From

In this chapter we will see the spaces from which we can create. The first ones that I explain are those that arise out of the consciousness of being in one's authentic and essential identity:

- *Non-violent space: Ahimsa*
- *Open space*
  - *Trust*
  - *Detachment*
  - *Freedom*
  - *Availability*
- *Space of acceptance*
  - *Forgiveness*
  - *Respect*
  - *Tolerance*
  - *Receptive*
  - *Surrender*
  - *Harmonization*
- *Space of abundance and generosity*
  - *Wholeness*
  - *Kind: Kalosini*
  - *Love*
  - *Beauty*
  - *Tenderness*
- *Empty space*
  - *What empty space?*
  - *Freedom*
  - *Universal*

- *Inclusive*
- *New*
- *Revision*
- *Space of silence*
  - *Truth*
  - *Reflection*
  - *Connection*
  - *Attention*
  - *Concentration*
  - *Contemplation*
- *Space of authenticity*
  - *Real and genuine*
- *Life-giving space of enthusiasm*
  - *Optimism*
  - *Vitality*
  - *Challenging the limits*
  - *Determination*
  - *Will*
  - *Being in love*

Then we will look at some of the spaces that arise out of the personality of the ego and that make up part of the old paradigm. From those spaces we sustain the worldwide situation of the ego-system in which there is injustice, great imbalances and differences between rich and poor. Some of these spaces are:

- *Space of loneliness and isolation*
- *Space of pain*
- *Space of anger*
- *Space of fear*
- *Space of inferiority and insecurity*

Creating space

The space that creativity arises out of is the laboratory from where you experience and discover in order to feel, live out, and express wholeness. It is a space from where you work, discover and experience. From there, you transmit what you are learning.

To create space is to allow the presence of the subtle, the invisible, the divine energy, to enter into your life and act, and, through you, to manifest in the world. It is to remain conscious, awake and to awaken others.

The inner space of the self is not conditioned by judgments, false beliefs or limitations. To be conscious of that space, we should be careful not to lose ourselves in the sensorial experiences that the senses offer us. When we get lost in any of these experiences, we forget the being that experiences, and we identify with pleasure or pain, with the image or the word. On identifying with it, we lose the broad and real vision of the self.

Sometimes we flee from our inner space, we are afraid of going inwards and seeing. Creativity comes out of the inner space. If you are disconnected from it, your creativity will come from the 'automatic pilot' of your habits or dependencies.

Feel the security of being safe to look within yourself, to look at your past, to broaden your vision, to recognize the magnificence of your being. Have the courage to leave the circle of security that you have installed yourself in. Explore your potential.

Once it has emerged and the creative act has occurred: 'the work' has been created, you have to take care so that the notion of *I* and *mine* does not emerge, so that you do not appropriate what you have made, since, if you do, the ego has returned and clouds up the space and its creation.

Let us see different characteristics and qualities of this inner space.

Non-violent space: Ahimsa

Ahimsa is more than peace. It is the total absence of violence. Complete non-violence.

In this space you feel accepted as you are.

It is a space that does not impose. It does not invade.

It is a space that generates harmony, peace, order and balance.

It is the space that joins the drop with the ocean. It joins the being with the Universe. This union is only possible out of non-violence, Ahimsa. See the subheading 'The power of the point', in the chapter, 'Universal creativity'.

It is the space that creates and allows other spaces of creation. From this space we will be able to create a true culture of peace.

Open space

Here the energy flows, it does not run aground, it does not get blocked, it does not leave its course, it does not get distorted.

It is a space of trust

We have to make it possible for there to be spaces of trust, spaces where each person can be themselves.

When we create from a base of self-esteem and self-respect we are more optimistic. From that state, we trust that we will find opportunities or that the opportunities will find us; we will find seeds charged with positive energy that can grow if we nurture them.

- You trust that the best is possible for you.
- You trust that the Universe brings to you what you need and what is best.
- You trust that what you need to know will be revealed to you.
- You trust that what you need will come to you.
- You trust in yourself, you believe in yourself and in your inner resources.

It is a space of detachment

Detachment facilitates and promotes creativity. Dependences

obstruct. Fear blocks.

Detachment is when you don't identify with the object of your creativity, with the idea that you have had, with the result or the form.

Without detachment, you impose. Your personality comes into action and you suffocate the other: you oppress them. Attachment prevents you from enjoying the essence itself of the thing or the person that you are attached to. The consciousness that appears in you is that of possessing or controlling, not that which corresponds to the object or subject possessed.

When you get too involved in a matter, a discussion, a disagreement, a clash or emotional pushing and pulling, you put all your energy into wanting to win, that matter is dominating your time in that moment; it dominates you and feeds off your personal power, it weakens you. While you participate in that matter, you are tied. And if, on top of that, you feel that the other person is the one that comes out winning, you feel defeated. Nevertheless, you continue to be stuck in your negative feelings on the matter, which means that your power continues to be weak.

Detachment arises out of the consciousness that nothing or nobody is 'mine'. It is a consciousness of freedom.

It is a space of freedom

You create something and you let it go, you let it have its own life, and you disappear. God is the greatest creator because He disappears and what appears is the creation. He creates and allows to be. If what you create attracts you, you need recognition. In detachment, you give power to what you create. In attachment, you take power from what you create. On letting go, you keep your personal power whole and your freedom.

It is a space in which there is availability

You are available to:

- Perceive energy from God.
- Listen to signs and act in consequence.
- Carry out the right action.
- You allow according to the need of the moment or the people (not of the I, I, I, egocentric and narcissist).

Space of acceptance

Accepting yourself is the key to beginning and carrying out any positive change. It implies approving of yourself, *self approval*.

It is to feel that you are in the right place, at the right time, doing the right thing. Out of acceptance you have changed certain beliefs. Before you believed that you had to make yourself strong in order to go out into the world; now you are in the world and you show yourself as you are, without the need to prove anything. Before you had a feeling of valuing yourself little; now you know where it comes from, you know there is no reason to have it and you no longer feel yourself to be less. You feel better.

You accept yourself and you express yourself from that acceptance, generating a space of acceptance for others who, in your presence, feel embraced, accepted and comfortable.

Out of the space of acceptance a different action is created.

It is a space of forgiveness

Jesus on the cross said: "Father, forgive them for they know not what they do." Only a great heart has such a level of forgiveness. In the space of acceptance, you broaden the limits of your heart.

It is a space of respect

You give space to receive what others can teach you or bring to you. You give space so that they can learn in their own time.

It is a space of tolerance

You accept the other as he is. You accept what he is.

It is important to understand that to overcome problems, you need, on the one hand, inner power, and on the other, the capacity to tolerate. To tolerate does not mean to put up with. To tolerate is to accept, understand and know how to face things. That is, to tolerate is not to put up with something and then explode. In tolerance you dissolve that which, otherwise, you would be putting up with. It is like the sea, which is an example of tolerance, because we throw a lot of dirt into the sea, the sea absorbs it and, with time, transforms it. Tolerance is to be like the ocean, that is, to know how to absorb and dissolve, to make disappear. You can find this developed at more length in the book *Dare to Live,* in the chapter that deals with tolerance.

It is a receptive space
It is a space of surrender

You go into it because you have learned to yield, to cede and to give yourself over. The important and interesting thing is that it is without submission and without being a victim. It supposes neither getting blocked nor putting up resistance. Resisting and blocking others or yourself would imply:

- Control.
- Fear.
- Insecurity.
- Opposition to what is.

To cede is to accept internally what you have, to be open to life. Resistance is an internal contraction, a hardening of the ego, it is to close oneself. As Tolle reminds us: **"Not to offer resistance is the key to accessing the greater power of the Universe."**

A new dimension of consciousness is opened up when you cede, when you yield. If it is possible to act, your action will be in harmony with the whole and supported by the creative intelligence, the consciousness with which you join in that state of openness. In that state coincidences happen, people and circumstances help you and accompany you on your following stage. If it is not possible to act, you remain with the inner calm that accompanies this state of yielding, of handing over and acceptance.

Another way of understanding surrender is connected to freedom, and the *Upanishads* tell us about it in an aphorism:

Freedom of the soul has no laws. It is a law unto itself.
Freedom is not over others; it is within yourself.
Freedom has no meaning if it is not for all.
The truly religious man is he whose soul is free for God.

It is a space of being in tune

Being in tune with what is. You accept what is and are in tune with what is. If you resist, you are not in tune, you do not perceive, you do not pick up on the signals that the situation or the other is giving you, and, therefore, you cannot give the best of yourself for a mutual benefit (yours and of the situation or other person/people).

When you act in tune with the present moment, your actions are impregnated with the wisdom of your innate being, of your soul.

Space of abundance and generosity

It is a space linked to wholeness, not to what is lacking in the ego. Because of this you don't feel guilt, and neither do you blame the other; in you there is neither resentment nor bitterness; neither addictive needs nor do you become a victim. You are not creative in order to satisfy your needs.

You cannot receive what you do not give. What you think the world denies you, you already have; you have to let it come out of you or, if not, you will not know that you have it. Jesus already gave us the key to this when he said: "For this reason I tell you, whatever you pray and ask for, believe that you have received it, and it will be yours" (Mark 11:24).

You are creative offering the best of yourself. You become a giver. You are generous, you trust in your inner abundance. On giving, you become aware of everything that lies within you. And, in each step that you take, you find wholeness.

Exercising leadership supposes removing obstacles, relieving the organizing system, trying not to de-motivate. Serving and not asking to be served. And this means generosity.

Generous creativity is natural, as it is in the tree and in the sun that illuminates and warms us generously. If the tree gets sick, it cannot give. Our illness is that of selfishness, resentment and hate. As Louise Hay says: "Resentment, criticism and guilt are the most damaging patterns." Out of those spaces there is no generosity, wholeness or abundance.

To enter into this space of abundance and generosity ask yourself often: what is it that I can offer, how can I contribute, what can I give? How can I serve in this situation?

It is not necessary to have anything to feel your abundance. On sharing from within yourself, the treasures that you carry within are awoken, and, as a result, you begin to receive in return everything that you need.

It is a space of wholeness
In which the following live:

- courage,
- bravery,
- enjoyment,
- contentment, and,
- happiness.

Here you trust that, if you lose something, if a situation or someone disappears or distances themselves from your life, this offers a space for something new to appear at the threshold of your being. You don't indulge yourself in a space of complaining or victim. You go forward.

Wholeness comes from the work being well done, with precision. It comes from the sincere work done from the heart and with honesty. It comes from simplicity and appreciating the simple in life.

It is a kind space

Kindness in Greek is *kalosini* and it means '**the natural goodness that flows from you**'. In abundance and generosity we don't expect anything from the other and then kindness flows from us to the other. Kindness is lost when you judge, criticize and have expectations. With all that you do not recognize the value of the other and you are not kind.

From the feeling of superiority you are not kind.

From inferiority you attract pity from others, not kindness.

The open space is a space of *love*. From this space you create bridges. In the opening *beauty* emerges, and the tenderness of your being.

It is a sweet place

In it you feel the sweetness, the harmony and the beauty of every-thing: you and the other, whether the other is a person, an animal, nature, God, the Universe.

Empty space
What empty space?

The more empty you feel your state of mind and your heart to be, the less creative you are, the more distractions you need and the more external stimuli. You lose yourself. You accumulate things in order to have a sensation of fullness. But you continue to feel an inner void. This feeling oneself to be in a void, without essence, without energy, is not the empty space I want to look at here.

The creative empty space is the one you create on letting go of dependences and cleaning memories of the past. You empty yourself of all that which invades your inner space and makes you feel grief, fear and bitterness. You empty yourself of bad feelings in order to thus generate a clean space. You empty yourself of the possessive 'I' and 'mine'. In this space the presence of the purest and most subtle energy can act and thus an unlimited creativity can burst forth.

It is a space of freedom
It is a space that is not conditioned.

That is why you can feel in the best way possible.

The freer you are, the less you expect perfection in others or around you. You stop being perfectionist.

You empty yourself of noisy judgments, of useless thoughts, of unnecessary feelings.

You are free of the 'I already know'.

It is the space of the self in the universal
In this space you are empty of the mistaken identification with the self, where the ego thinks and controls. With 'I do', it is the ego that does, and with 'I say', the ego is stuck onto the idea and the word.

You are empty of the 'me', in which I identify with my things, my role, my ideas, my creation. You let go of the limiting images that you have of yourself or that others have of you.

You are empty of the *mine*, of the mistaken sense of possession and possessiveness, of identifying yourself with objects, with people, with properties.

You are empty of the clinging on to *my* religion, *my* country, *my* culture, *my* politics. This clinging on is excluding. My religion, my country, my culture, my politics can be fantastic and marvelous; they form part of my roots, but clinging on to them turns me into a person who excludes others. Clinging on is at the root of conflicts.

In the empty space you do not exclude. You become a universal being. There is room for everyone in your space. **You do not separate, you join, you do not exclude, you include.**

- In this empty space the identification of the self changes.
- I am: supported in values, principles and beliefs (those that do not limit us).
- I am: I work on my attitudes and states of mind. I am prepared to overcome my differences and to improve my capacities with optimism, hope and trust.
- I have: I will work with the support of other people and my capacities.
- I can: I work on my competences that allow me to make progress.

The empty space is the space for the new

It is an empty space that allows for there to be newness.

On emptying yourself, you create space for the new.

That way God and Nature can inspire you. You have space!

From this empty space you can do something creative, transformative and new.

People are 'stuffed' and so full to overflowing that they cannot be authentically creative, because there is no space.

Space of revision

Every night revise yourself, and empty your mind, pack up all the happenings of the day, giving thanks for what you have learned. Empty your head of useless matters. Empty your heart of bad feelings, of unhealthy, bitter feelings. That way your rest will be reparative, your dreams will be a massage and you will wake up full of energy and vitality, without the burden of worries from the previous day.

The natural state of the mind is to be empty, clean and silent.

Space of silence

Silence is the space of the *truth*. It does not need justifications or demonstrations. Anthony Strano explains it as follows:

If I am aware of the truth, I remain silent.
Genuine truth proves itself in the course of time.
Corrections, proofs, insistence
are never points of revealing truth.
Often they are masks,
camouflaging personal irritation and bias.

It is a space of reflection

In silence, and with concentration, the circuits in your brain calm down and you are focused on your capacity to invent and reinvent yourself. In that space you have an unlimited creativity and **you can achieve the mental state that you want to**. The right question appears which will allow you to find the answer that you now need.

As Strano tells us:

I am learning to ask questions and let go of wanting answers.
When I am too focused on answers, I lose them.
Relevant questions are like brooms
that sweep the mind and create a clean space.
The mind needs clean space.
Answers enter clean space.
Now I start finding the essentials.

It is a space of connection

You connect to the room behind your eyes, to the space where all your creative energy resides. This connection allows you to rule in your life and channel your energy from your control cabin.

You connect to all your potential.

You connect to the essential.
You connect to your dream.
You connect to your purpose.
You connect to the Divine.

It is a space of attention

The attention is centered on the present. Feeling the presence of your being, with this energy, you impregnate what you do and you transform it.

Attention is the key to being able to transform.

As the musician pays attention to each note.

As the poet pays attention to each word.

In this space you learn to take care of things, to take care of the details.

Sometimes life presents you with something to get your attention; it is a call so that you will listen to a message. They are events that take place, or the body shouts at you to listen inside of yourself and stop repressing, fearing, hiding from what your being and life want to tell you.

Sometimes an intuition appears and we do not know what to do with it. We don't pay attention to it, we think it is nothing and this valuable information is diluted and lost. Anything that you give attention to in your life grows and is lit up.

Joe Dispenza explains to us that if we do not manage to think beyond our emotions, we will live according to what the environment orders for our body. Instead of thinking, innovating and creating, we will do no more than activate the synaptic memories of other areas of the brain according to our genetic inheritance or our personal past; we will continue in the routine. We will be at the mercy of the effect instead of being the creators of the cause. **Attention is the key to changing this automatic functioning**.

Our attention allows us to direct our energy towards what we want to. But, we should be careful! Attention, will and concentration have to go hand in hand. What happens is that sometimes, without being conscious, we fix our attention on the future or we anchor it in the past. Then, instead of being our best gift, it becomes our curse.

How to change this automatism? In the silence you reconnect to that to which you want to pay attention, you get back strength in order to put your decision into practice and direct your energy towards what is really important for you, without allowing your old habits to come back and dominate you and have power over you. Attention allows you to carry on being yourself while you rule in your life. You show your will when you choose to concentrate your attention. Often the stimuli around you distract you. Taking control and being attentive allows you to free yourself from those multiple influences.

Paying attention to the emerging of your essence and your values in your daily activities will help you to stay connected to the best of yourself. Sometimes what happens is that we have fixations and our attention is diverted and vitalizes our functioning of the ego character, disorienting our intuition and hiding our essence. A diverted mental attention happens when you perceive reality through acquired prejudices or through the experience acquired based on the ego character.

A diverted attention is influenced by the ego itself which, for example, tries to find the things that are wrong and what has to be changed; either it pays attention to receiving the approval of the other, or to obtaining recognition; it fixes onto the imperfections or what is lacking in the moment; it is attentive to keeping its privacy; it pays attention to trying to discover what is hidden, to discover the hidden intentions. Why is he saying this to me? It is alert to detecting the sources of power or authority. Paying attention while influenced by our ego makes it difficult for us to see the reality and have an objective observation.

In this space of silence, the attention is connected to your

intuition and to your spiritual and authentic essence.

It is a space of concentration

Concentration is the tool with which to go into the depth and dive into the Ocean of wisdom.

Concentration is the tool with which to create newness.

In concentration, thought is focused and centered, which means that mental chatter and other noises and distractions disappear. In that focusing, new experiences appear before you, you renew your vision and you broaden your horizons. The will and the capacity to reinvent yourself emerge.

With concentration you overcome addiction. As Joe Dispenza explains, "The main reason why most people cannot use their capacity for change is that they have become too addicted to their feelings and bodily emotions."

The same author tells us that we only learn when we concentrate our conscious perception deliberately on the chosen information using our free will. As human beings, we have the privilege of choosing where to direct our attention and for how long.

It is a space of contemplation

You have abandoned your hurries, the noises, the tasks and you are, you stay, in silence, in contemplation. There, everything becomes *one.* You feel part of the Universe and the Universe forms part of you. All your being is calm, opening, and from there flows the purest energy of your being.

Strano invites us to this space of contemplation:

In silence I anchor my being
And focus on the Divine,
and I absorb the blessing of the Truth,
which gives me the courage to make the necessary changes
without flinching, without excuse, without show.

"You don't co-operate,"
"You don't listen,"
"You don't understand,"
"I am not valued enough,"
are all accusations and demands of the narcissistic mind,
which eventually finds itself unheard, unwanted, alone.
It remains such,
until that instant when the mind opens
and wants to be with God.

Space of authenticity
It is a real and genuine space

Here emerges the truth of your being.
You are in the center of your essence.
You are sincere and honest.
You no longer flee.
You don't hide.
You are complete.

In the space of authenticity you do not devote yourself to purifying your external expression, with your talents and skills, looking for a false authenticity. In authenticity you do not look to improve or embellish the masks in order to keep escaping or hiding. That would be to falsify. To show a self that is not.

You have the wish and the willingness to see yourself as you are. You accept yourself. You don't beat yourself up. You do not oppress or repress.

Swami Amar Jyoti explains how to enter into the space of authenticity:

Don't you see? Don't be afraid any more. Don't be a stranger any more. Don't hide any more. Simply see the whole and know. And here, now it's suddenly safe enough. It's suddenly clear enough, there is suddenly love enough to dare to let go, to relax, to open to Him and let Him show us – what? Ourselves. Our True Self!

Vital space of enthusiasm

When you are excited by your mission, your work, your life project, when you are excited by what you can offer life, what life offers you, you wake up each morning with an unlimited reserve of energy and enthusiasm.

The etymology of the word *enthusiasm* comes from the Greek 'in Zeus', 'to have God with you'. It is not surprising, then, that enthusiasm instills a great force into everything you do. What is more, you discover that you don't have to do it alone: the presence of the life energy, of the divine energy, acts in and through you, inspiring you towards co-operation, creating synergy. Sustained enthusiasm brings a wave of creative energy to existence.

Enthusiasm arises out of an energy of vitality, that opposes nothing, it does not confront; rather, it flows, overcomes, speeds up, moves, channels and creates.

It is a space of optimism

The impossible seems possible.

You see it as possible.

You don't wear blinkers. From this space you see the complete panorama, with an open attitude for all possibilities.

You are full of vitality

In this space there is ease and lightness, which makes it easy for the energy to move and flow.

It is a space that elevates the energy and maintains it on a high vibration.

It is a space which challenges the limits

Each person, basing themselves on their beliefs, establishes the limits of how their life manifests itself. With enthusiasm, you challenge your own limits. You cause things to go well in the direction that you want.

In this space, blockages do not exist, not even in your vocabulary.

Everything that happens is a step to move oneself forward and to go upward. Whatever comes, you progress, you advance and you ascend. You stay motivated.

It is a space with determination

This space gives you the power.

The power of decision.

The power of focusing.

The power of will.

Your energy is channeled and centered on the action.

It is a space with will

What you believe you should do and what you feel you want to do are aligned.

You discern and you prioritize.

You see it, you believe it, you feel it and you get passionate about it.

You have the will of being: what you want and what you don't want.

You have the will of effort, of doing, of achieving, of fighting for. You have the will to oblige yourself to do that which the reason determines but that the feeling tries to avoid or vice versa.

From here the capacity emerges to do what you set out to do.

It is a space of being in love

Love is a powerful motivator.

If you fall in love with your ideal, you will join with a new version of yourself. The power of falling in love is what unites. It unites you to the other. In this case, the other is your ideal, your dream, your objective.

Joe Dispenza advises us that:

We should be in love with our new vision, not ever get tired or bored of it. We should always feel the need to be with this new concept, to visit it often. The vision that we want to create of ourselves should awaken in us the same feeling as when we are in love for the first time, when the object of our affection seems to us the incarnation of all that is pure and true.

With enthusiasm you dare to aim higher and your energy moves positively and passionately to bring you closer to your vision.

Creating from the old paradigm

There are other spaces from which we create. They are spaces of the old paradigm: of the ego, of the defense mechanisms of the self, of the false identities of the self. Spaces of the self that are asleep and have not woken up to their true being. Knowing that when we create from these spaces we are creating from our limited self helps us to recognize the road that we still have to cover. It is a help that acts as a mirror; it allows you to see yourself and to see where you are.

I am going to look briefly at some of those spaces:

Space of loneliness and isolation
Space of pain
Space of anger
Space of fear
Space of inferiority and insecurity
Space of loneliness and isolation
What do you create out of this space?
Feelings of being alienated and isolated.
Pessimism.
Depression.

Despair.

Lament.

Anguish.

You feel trapped.

You feel misunderstood.

You feel abandoned.

You feel rejected, not accepted, not loved.

Sometimes you shout to be heard, because you believe that nobody wants to listen to you.

You get ill so that you will be looked after because you believe that nobody wants to look after you.

Feeling alone generates an anguish that is sometimes unbearable. We have the alternative of fleeing from the responsibility that freedom offers us, generating different forms of dependency and submission, or rather of carrying on until the complete realization of freedom, reaching wholeness and personal development, and enjoying solitude in its fullness. I write about this in the book *Dare to Live*.

Some suggestions to get out of the space of loneliness

Recognize that loneliness is self-imposed. There are many people who would be delighted to enjoy your company.

Open yourself! And receive from the abundance that the Universe has ready to give you.

Dare to commit yourself. Without commitment you don't regain the strength to come out of isolation. When you commit yourself, Providence also acts. To help you, all kinds of things happen that, without your decision and without your commitment, would not happen. Daring makes your strengths emerge. Start now!

Space of pain

Emotional pain and mental pain lead us to illness. In reality, according to Eric Rolf, neither illnesses nor ill people exist; what exists is communication. The only exception is the illness of spiritual deafness.

Life speaks to us in whispers. If we do not listen, it speaks louder to us; if we still don't know how to understand or we don't want to listen, it continues to speak to us louder and louder until it shouts. That shout is pain, illness or an accident.

Destructive suffering, that from which we don't take away any learning whatsoever, will not bring us anything. It will only make it easy for us to adopt certain victim positions.

There is a suffering that Gurdjieff calls the "suffering with meaning", the creative pain, that drives us to change, to transformation, to being humble and to having compassion for the other. Here I deal with the space of destructive and unhealthy pain. In the subheading 'What is the incentive for transformation?' I deal with that creative suffering.

What do you create from this space?

Separation.
Blockage.
Self-pity.
Illness.
Grief.
Revenge.
Resentment.

One can even become a hypochondriac: anything makes one ill.

Enmity. The ego feels the pain. The force that pushes the desire of the ego creates enemies. You react with an opposed force of the same intensity, somatizing the unhappiness in relationships. This multiplies the pain.

Some suggestions to get out of the space of pain

The pain that arises out of a loss and, during the process of grieving, requires us to be aware that to live trapped in the memory of a loved one who left us, in the memory of a situation that no longer exists, or in the memory of someone who lives but who we no longer see (we have separated physically) does not allow us to enjoy ourselves freely in the present moment.

To live through the mourning and overcome it is to have the capacity to make peace with the memories recorded on our memory. It is to reach a point when they do not disturb us or generate pain in us. It is to reach a point that the memory of what was and no longer is does not generate desires, dissatisfaction, frustration or sadness.

We do not get over our grieving for a loved one, a lost child, a disappeared love, because we allow the memory to continue alive in such a way that it invades our consciousness and colonizes our spirit. The memory suffocates the present, wanting to relive a past that can no longer exist. It is over.

Grieving is to free oneself of the known and lived. It is to cut the strings or ties of the attachment to that past experience. (I deal with this subject in the book, *Live in Freedom*).

- *Trust*. We have been born with the capacity to live, whatever happens, in a non-traumatic form. We are always ready to deal with any challenge that we are presented with. If life brings it to us, we are prepared for it. It is not only that we can overcome it, but that in some way it supports us on our path. Discover this truth.
- *Understand*. On the path there are always challenges; they are not there to cause us trauma, but so that we can continue evolving.
- *Create* a **space of health** when the body speaks to you through pain, unhappiness: understanding the code of the body, the inner creative language that communicates something to us through bodily and emotional pain. Understand what belief, what learning, what the message is that you have to listen to. Understanding the inner communication accelerates healing and gives you the possibility of letting go of the pain. If you need help to do

it, go to a doctor of the soul.

We all have healing power in us. It is the same energy and the same power that has created the illness and the pain. You can use that power to heal yourself by channeling it in another way.

Be aware.

Listen to the message that pain brings you.

Eric Rolf encourages us by saying:

Listen to your inner voice and pay attention to it. Not listening to it is the beginning of the creation of illness. Our own beliefs are those which prevent us from living out or showing that part that we do not listen to, which continues to grow, albeit unconsciously. This growth does not have a physical expression, since we do not allow it to. The illness or physical problem is the physical expression of that part, which is an unconscious way of living out our path.

Acquire more knowledge in order to increase your under-standing.

Love others. Accompany your neighbor. Leave this space of pain and serve others. Connect to your inner Vishnu (see page 92).

Detach yourself and let go of the pain: don't cling onto it. It is not yours. You are free.

Listen to your intuition. The appearance of a symptom is the result of a process that begins on not allowing ourselves to express a part of us. Rolf explains to us that a symptom is an unconscious expression; paying attention to our intuition directly supports the process of healing, because it allows us to find a way out of that inner part that is not through a symptom.

Take a 'multivitamin tablet', that is, use your inner powers and essential values together in order to leave the space of pain.

You can read the book *Live in Freedom*, where some of the

subjects I deal with are useful for leaving the space of pain.

According to an aphorism of the *Upanishads*, pain is the product of your ignorance:

There is not a single misery in the world which is real.

There is not a single pain on the whole earth which is created by the Creator.

Any pain in your life is due to separateness, or misconception of separateness from the Creator.

There is no real pain and misery involved, if you take it from the Creator's viewpoint, the cosmic view.

Space of anger

Violence is a form through which the ego tries to affirm itself, to show that it is right. It wants to dominate, control, have power and be the strongest. The greater the lack of awareness in individuals or groups, the easier it is to adopt a position of violence.

Anger can show itself as impatience, irritation, frustration, criticism, resentment, jealousy or bitterness. All thoughts created from that space act as poison in the body.

Resentment, criticism and guilt are patterns of thoughts, feelings and words that harm and generate illness. The resentment increases the more you blame. With resentment you keep yourself in the space of continuing to blame.

What do you create from this space?

- You create *hate*.
- You create *revenge*.
- You create *rage*.
- You 'un-create', you destroy.
- You create enmity.
- You create grief.
- You create bad feelings.
- You create fear in others.

- You create distance.
- You create conflict.
- You create dissatisfaction.
- You create dryness: your love, your tenderness dries up.

Some suggestions in order to get out of the space of anger

Anger, whether you repress or you direct it at someone, damages you. If you feel anger, the way to express it is to observe it from within you, as something external. To dissolve it, you can write down your feelings, draw them or paint them, run or dance, in such a way as to relieve your body and your heart of that energy of anger without projecting it onto anybody.

Let us look at other suggestions for overcoming anger:

- Let go.
- Let go of the expectations that you had, because, on them not being fulfilled, you get irritated. The problem is not in your expectations not being fulfilled. The problem is in your expectations. Let go of them. Accept what is. Do not try to control others. Control your reactions.
- Let go of the past.
- Un-harden and soften the self, which does not mean to weaken the self, but rather soften yourself by being lighter, by letting go of burdens.
- Create a space of forgiveness. Forgive everyone, including yourself.
- Practice the advice of Zen: do not look for the truth, simply abandon your opinions. You do not need justifications.
- Allow others to be.
- Learn, value the learning of experience, don't hold on to resentment. That way you will be able to be grateful for having had it.
- Don't blame yourself.
- Don't feel yourself to be a victim. Don't entertain feelings

like these: you did this to me and for that I hate you and I want to get revenge, you will pay for it.

- Be kind.

Anger is a strong energy that moves people, relationships, and the world. It is the cause of a multitude of disasters, destruction, mistreatment, violence and death. It is what makes the mind go mad. Let us learn to channel this potent energy by turning it into compassion. The passion of understanding the other, of communicating out of love, of living in communion and not in separation.

Space of fear

What do you create from this space?

Tension, anxiety, nervousness, insecurity, worries, doubts, not feeling good enough, not being up to things, you feel unworthy.

You create more fear, sadness, anger and confusion.

Fear causes subjugation, dependence and addiction.

Ignorance and lack of knowledge lead us to fear.

Some suggestions to get out of the space of fear

In order to heal, we should substitute fear for trust and faith. Faith in life. If you say *yes* to the Universe, then life and the Universe say *yes* to you.

Trust that your body is already ready for the adventure of your soul.

In the book *Dare to Live*, I deal with the subject of fears at depth and how to regain your inner power, your bravery, trust and wholeness. For example, one of the things you will find in that book is that there are some fears that are overcome with the practice of doing that which you are afraid of, as long as it is something positive and valid. If you do not take the brave step of overcoming the fear of expressing yourself, you will continue to be the victim of this fear that disorganizes your ideas and makes you lose the thread when you are speaking.

It is important to take on the commitment of recognizing, managing and overcoming our fears, because, if not, we ourselves will be the victims of our mental and emotional ignorance.

Space of inferiority and insecurity

What do you create from this space?

In this space you submit yourself to the erroneous sense of identity that you have of yourself.

You create feelings of incapacity.

You look for praise and affirmation.

You need approval.

You need recognition.

Others feel sorry for you.

You create submission to others.

You compare yourself to others.

You undervalue yourself.

It is difficult for you to co-operate with others.

You find it difficult to participate.

You are afraid. You close yourself in. You doubt. You feel yourself a martyr. You tremble.

Some suggestions for getting out of the space of inferiority and insecurity

- Respect towards yourself based on knowing your true value.
- Detachment from the idea that you have of yourself. You are not the idea. It is your perception, but it is not you.
- Humility. Humility is to have courage and be open to the learning that another can bring you. When you have the humility to see your weaknesses, courage enters.
- Be open to see yourself and value yourself.
- Not see yourself through others' eyes.
- See yourself through the vision that God has of you: with

that elevated vision of yourself.

- Leave your egotism and give yourself to others.

12

From Theory to Practice, From Intention to Experience

In this chapter we will realize that we are clear about the theories but, in practice, the reality is totally different. Our addictions and habits are such that, although we want to, we cannot or we do not know how to do it. We feel that the cost of change is too much. And we keep ourselves where we are. Although we would like not to be there. Recognizing this is in itself an act of bravery. It is the first step.

To create a new reality, this newness has to arise out of a new mind, a new being with new attitudes and new values. Perhaps, if we analyze the values, they don't seem new, given that for some decades already we have been talking about them in lectures, conferences, congresses and meetings, through NGOs without frontiers, international bodies, foundations and associations.

What happens is that, often, they are not practiced in either our personal life nor that of relationships. We are not the change that we want to see in the world. Saint Paul already said it: "For I do not do the good I want, but I do the very evil I do not want!" (Romans 7:19). We have created formulas based on substituting some beliefs for others. We think that we take them to our practical life, but we do not feel them or practice them: it stays on the level of simply being a belief. Our lifestyles continue to be unsustainable. We continue on the old path, in the old forms.

It is likely that you, as a reader, make up part of the 5% of privileged people of the planet; that you can read, write, you have access to the newspaper, a roof over your head, running water and enough food. Congratulations. Now the question is: how much energy do you consume? How much do you throw away? How sustainable is your lifestyle? How much harmony is there in your life? How responsible are you? How conscious are you of your responsibility and your capacity to be a transforming and creative agent of a new world?

For example, you might think that you are loving and even preach love, but, observing what happens in your personal life, you can see that there is neither coherence nor practice. You realize that from the belief and the theory to the practice and the experience there is a stretch of uncovered ground. You have let yourself be carried away by emotional entropy, by the biological imperatives that govern the body. The dreams of a different future stay stifled under the feelings connected to the cycles of bodily, chemical, neuronal and emotional addiction feedback.

Aligning our intentions with our acts, pairing up our thoughts with our actions, leads to our personal evolution and, hence, to the collective evolution. What is more, that way you become a coherent example and inspiration for others to do the same and to realize that it is possible, that it is feasible. It is a question of deciding it and doing it without allowing yourself to be defeated by excuses or fears.

Often we devote ourselves to patching things up, but the crack continues growing and the wound doesn't heal. The old no longer works. The beliefs become outdated because we evolve, they are like a suit that has gotten too small for us. The focus on the past makes us rigid. We have to be flexible in all directions. When one believes that one is being flexible, it is possible that it is only in one direction.

Experiencing a change is like abandoning all the known things and memories. It is to create from the present and from the vision of the future.

Attention, the will and concentration are absolutely necessary in order to carry out the change that we want in our life. To overcome the inner resistance to change, we should dare to go to the other shore, as I explained in the chapter, 'How to Live Creatively in a Chaotic World'.

Perhaps what we need is spiritual alchemy and some creative guidelines.

13

Spiritual Alchemy

Life is magic, don't miss out on it.

Alchemy is magic transformation, metamorphosis. You don't know exactly what happens but, on combining a series of elements, a miracle takes place, an unexpected gift, the veil is un-veiled and a marvelous truth is revealed that opens your wings to fly to another dimension.

In this chapter we will see these subheadings:

- *Spiritual alchemy*
- *The Sakash*
- *The Mansa Seva*
  - *In the service of madness*
  - *A mind qualified to serve*
  - *Mind and heart united*
  - *Serving through the mind*
- *The Drishti*
- *Synergy*
- *The miracle*
- *Grace*
- *The mystery*
- *The power of zero*

I use some words in Sanskrit because a word contains a global meaning, broad and of profound significance. It enriches us.

Spiritual alchemy

The alchemist attempts to transform metals — like lead — into gold. He works in his laboratory combining chemical products and using the energy of fire. As alchemists, we can turn our life into a laboratory in order to transform that which weighs us down, the lead of our life, into gold: flexible, shining, valuable.

Spiritual alchemy uses the non-physical in the physical world; it uses metaphysical energy in the physical and bodily dimension. That non-physical energy would be the fire, the energy of the awakened consciousness that opens itself to the divine, to the fire of pure love. The physical would be situations and realities in the day-to-day, the chemical elements that we have to combine in our life.

For example when a good friend looks into your eyes and transports you to a space of tenderness and acceptance, in an instant your fears are dissolved. The metaphysical energy of the consciousness has acted through the look.

For example when a doctor or a person who is a good carer takes your hand and transmits to you a healing energy that feeds your hope. In that contact there has been alchemy.

They are moments in which an energy of another quality enters and acts in you. Those moments can happen in the contemplation of nature, in prayer, in contact with someone, in the silence and the quiet brought about by an illness, and in other sporadic and apparently casual moments. However, they happen often when the awakening of the consciousness arrives.

When your consciousness awakens, you realize that the energy that moves the world no longer moves you. The energy of consumerism, of being in a hurry, of selfishness, of forcing things, of repressing or of oppressing, no longer moves you. Another energy begins to act in you: the non-physical light, the subtle, the energy of love, of the soul, of the pure feelings and of the feelings connected to the essential.

In spiritual alchemy we find the *Sakash*; the *Mansa Seva*; the *Drishti*; synergy; the miracle; grace; the mystery and the power of zero acting.

Sakash: the light and the divine power

Sakash is a Sanskrit word. It refers to the light and the divine might that acts in you and through you.

The light is clarity, wisdom, discernment.

The might is elevated energy, of a high vibratory level, pure and purifying, concentrated and clean.

It is the energy capable of dissolving patterns, addictions and habits. The *Sakash* purifies and elevates.

It comes from God.

When the *Sakash* acts in you, you can share with others the power of love and co-operation, you can give them an experience of peace, of rest and of tranquility. And all of this in a short time. You open others to this experience, without the necessity of speaking. Your vibration and your presence are transforming. You awaken others with the light and power of your presence.

Mansa Seva

In Hindu it means 'a mind that serves'. *Seva* is 'service'. *Man* is 'mind'.

Mansa Seva is to help through thought. The language of thought travels and reaches the other. If the energy of the mobile telephone arrives through space at the other end of the world, why would our thoughts not have the power to reach the other? The other can absorb that energy and vibration.

When thoughts are united with the power of pure, not negative, feelings, they will make the other feel lighter. They will help them to lighten themselves of burdens.

If what you send through your radar are bad feelings and negative thoughts, these act like the force of gravity: they knock the other down; they give them a headache; they feel distress and go into themselves to defend themselves from that energy that reaches them.

In the service of madness

For the *Mansa Seva* you should have a mind that is qualified to serve. There are many that, in the present day, have dysfunctional minds that create and sustain the madness in the world. They are minds absorbed in *maya:* the illusory veil (according to the writings of India), falsity, **what is not but appears to be.**

The mind is intelligent, but the intelligence is affected by madness and foolishness. It has been capable of creating destruction on the planet and people. Throughout history, humans have suffered more at the hands of other humans than through natural disasters.

Intelligence has been used in the service of madness. In 1914, with the First World War, the intelligent human mind had already invented bombs, machine guns, submarines, poisonous gases. In a few years more than ten million human beings died. Many were mutilated. On seeing the devastation, the horror was enormous. However, few suspected that that was only the beginning. Afterwards came the Holocaust, the assassination of millions of 'class enemies and traitors' in Stalin's Soviet Union. Civil wars, like the Spanish one. Killings like in Cambodia, etc. Watching the news, we see how the intelligence and the mind in the service of madness continues in full activity.

A mind qualified to serve

A mind in the service of madness cannot be of any use except for destruction. So – we should learn to think again!

Let us develop the skill of cultivating high quality thoughts.

The *Mansa Seva* functions like when we magnetize a bar of iron. You don't have to magnetize each cell of that bar for it to become a magnet. You only need the square root of one per cent. In the same way, what is needed with this kind of subtle service through the mind is that enough people begin to serve with elevated thoughts, pure feelings and benevolent actions to set in motion a sweeping transformation of the world.

Dadi Janki reminds us that in these times, when we see the conditions of the world, many of us want to serve the world. But when our minds become affected by the conditions of the world, we cannot really serve. A mind full of anger or sadness cannot serve.

We cannot give to the world when we feel ourselves to be weakened by the heaviness of the world and by the atmosphere of a tired world. We can only give to others when we have reclaimed our spiritual power.

For the boat to reach its destination, the water should stay out of the boat. For our minds to be able to serve, the atmosphere of the world should stay outside of our minds. The atmosphere of the outside should not penetrate into the boat of our mind, but rather the opposite – the vibrations of a powerful and clean mind should influence the atmosphere outside, strengthening those that live in the world.

To have a mind capable of healing the world first we have to heal ourselves, cultivating healing powers such as hope, harmony, compassion, commitment, forgiveness, tolerance and respect.

When we fill ourselves with the power of spirituality, we emanate it continuously. We create each thought and each feeling with a beneficial and serving intention. When the world has enough people with a mind of this quality, then the new world, the golden age, will come, bringing peace and light to the world.

Mind and heart united
Mansa Seva is to serve with the mind, but the mind is deeply connected to the heart. The mind creates thoughts and the heart, feelings. If a thought arises but that feeling is not there in my heart, how can I serve? Or, if there is a feeling but not the thought, how can it work?

Service is given through sincerity, compassion and the feelings of love. The heart desires to do something. It feels that it is necessary to do this.

Serve through the mind

Dadi Janki explains that there are three kinds of service through the mind:

- To serve with feelings of love and mutual respect for the one who already has a close relationship with God and is awake.
- To serve with feelings of love and support for those who feel weak.
- To serve with feelings of love and compassion for those who believe they do not need any help at all.

The Drishti

It is the power of seeing that arises out of the consciousness of the awakened soul. The eyes are the window of the soul. In the Drishti the eyes have recovered their shine and:

- You see the other as your brother.
- You see the other as a person with a right to be here, and to be as they are.
- You see their eternal value and their dignity.
- You see the heart of their being.

Through the *Drishti* you transmit the *Sakash* to the other person. On looking, you see the being naked of labels, beyond the form, and your energy rises and raises that of the other.

Synergy

The etymology of the Greek word *synergasia* means 'together for the task'.

It is the power of joining and uniting.

In synergy, you are co-operative in differences.

Conflicts are resolved out of synergy and a mutual agreement is reached, mutual understanding. Understanding becomes natural.

In synergy, 1 + 1 is not 2, rather they multiply. And in that increase of energy what seemed impossible becomes possible.

The miracle

This is not a book about miracles. However, it seems necessary to me to mention them, since they are part of the results of spiritual alchemy.

The miracle is something extraordinary that appears in your life when you couldn't even imagine it. It comes to you from beyond your expectations.

It is real, but you cannot explain it with words. It is beyond the explicable, beyond the why, the what, the who, even the how.

The miracle can reach you through faith and effort. When you don't cover over the world with words and labels, the sense of the miraculous returns to your life, a perception that was lost some time ago. Depth returns to your life. Things recover their newness, their freshness. And then the greatest miracle occurs, according to Tolle: you experience your essential self before words, before ideas, mental labels and images. The creativity that flows from this experience will generate spaces of miraculous transformation

Grace

Grace is something extra, a gift given by God. You have not had to work to receive it. Your intention is good, and the grace of God helps you.

It depends on your intention and attitude, of you being open to receive it.

If your attitude is clear, your intention clean and your heart is open, you receive the grace of God.

The act of grace is the start of the process of awakening: there is not a clear sequence of logical steps that take you there, although the mind would love it to be like that. It occurs, like an 'aha' moment, like a flash that touches your heart and opens it to an awakening from which emerge pure feelings of universal love.

The mystery

In Greek, *mysterion* can mean 'symbol', 'secret', 'mystery that reveals itself'. You have to know how to decipher the symbols to understand the mystery they contain. We should know how to listen to the secret that is communicated or explained through symbols or words (which are also symbols) with the 'third ear', the ear of the soul. The mystery that is revealed is a secret project that was hidden and is now revealed. The veil is removed and one can see with the inner eye, the third eye, the eye of the heart of the soul, which sees that which is invisible to the eyes of the body.

We lose the mystery of life, of God, of His grace, of the supreme intelligence and of so many things, because we cover over the mystery with labels, we want to know it and we rationalize it, we analyze it and we give it a name. On giving it a name we limit it, we close it in. We put a veil over it and what we imagine that there is behind the veil is not the reality of the mystery, but our projection and fantasy.

The label of tree, the name, oak, does not signify that we discover it or experience its beauty. The dawn, the clouds, and so many other things, such as a look, a smile, a gesture, make up part of the mystery of life, of the constant exchange of energy that we lose because we are not conscious of it. We remain trapped in the phenomenon and we fail to see the reality.

The power of zero

The power of zero manifests itself when you put one thing right and many others then put themselves right automatically. You don't have to make an effort for each thing. You straighten up one and others follow.

You go through a process that brings and generates many benefits.

It is not 1 + 1 + 1. You put yourself at the 0 and then the rest puts itself into place.

The power of zero is the subtle energy of the divine that works through time and space and transcends it.

The power of zero is the symbol of the power of nothing, of feeling oneself nothing because you surrender, you give in, you hand yourself over. It is the power that can work on the negative patterns and the ego of the person when they surrender and give themselves over to this experience (see 'Empty Space', page 124).

The power of zero arises out of the energy of silence, the divine energy that comes to the bodily world of time, space, sound and relationships. If you open your receptacle, it enters into you and comes out of you. You have to be a good receptacle, a good receiver. Don't allow your ego to interfere. We don't pick up on it because the sun does not reach the covered flower.

We cover ourselves with:

- Resentment.
- Guilt.
- Comparisons.

And we do not pick up on the subtle energy and that immense love that it radiates. It is an energy of love that cares, that caresses, that elevates.

The power of zero is the creative intelligence joined to the whole, to the higher order.

The power of zero appears when, in action, you participate and cooperate. You are *one* with what you do and that way you contribute to the construction of the new world.

The power of zero when you cannot act materializes in that:

- You rest in the silence.

- You observe.
- You feel.
- You enjoy.
- You delight.
- You marvel.
- You wait. You don't get nervous.
- You are, and your presence remains. You act out of the silence and quietness. You practice the *Mansa Seva*.

14

Plan for Being: Creative Guidelines

After seeing all the dimensions of creativity that I have set out for you, the spaces from which you can create and the transformation that you can generate, the question is: what are you going to do now? I suggest that you set out to have a creativity that maintains your personal power: the *Sakash*, the *Mansa Seva*, the *Drishti*, Vishnu. That way you will keep your energy at the highest level. You will maintain your inner strength, your essence and your integrity. That way you will trust and believe in yourself.

This level of commitment melts down the weaknesses and you are ready; your energies flow.

You have to put it to yourself, you have to want to, you have to take the decision, have the will and do it. *Now*. Commit yourself and act. *Dare* to **commit yourself**. Commit yourself in a decided way to the practice of new attitudes, thoughts and actions.

Goethe described the results of commitment thus:

Until you commit yourself, there is the doubt, the possibility of turning back, always without benefits. In relation to all acts of initiative (and creation), there is an elemental truth the ignorance of which kills an endless number of ideas, as well as splendid plans: that in the moment that one truly commits oneself, Providence also acts. To help us, all kinds of things happen that, without decision, would never happen. A whole stream of happenings come from the decision, causing, in our favor, all kinds of unforeseen incidents, encounters and material help that nobody would have ever dreamed could happen. Anything that you can dream that you can do, start doing it. The daring carries with it genius, power and magic. Start now!

You can **ask yourself**:

- What do I want for myself?
- Why and for what do I exist?
- What is life asking of me?
- What is it offering me to do?

Clarify your goals. For example, you can have the goal of creating the best in yourself, offering the best of yourself.

Being curious about everything that happens within you and everything that surrounds you, not accepting as right and acceptable the automatic answers that your ego character gives to your questions. Always seek your inner truth, and what is authentic outside, in order not to let yourself be carried away by mirages.

Other questions that you can ask yourself in order to keep your **inner observer** awake are:

- What do I do? Or what am I doing?
- What do I pay attention to?
- What am I focusing on?
- What calls for my attention?
- Am I present or absent, carried away by my attention?

Being in the present in this moment strengthens your essence. On observing, you can redirect your attention.

Affirmations can be a method to fulfill your goals. They are a good seed, but they are not enough, because you need to plant them in real life, water them and feed them daily.

You also have to **cover over the holes** of the bucket, of the receptacle of your mind where there are leakages of energy. That way, when you water yourself with the knowledge of your being and you nourish yourself with good feelings, the bucket is filled and you can share out the water with generosity, as the gardener does.

Give space to your life

It is good to give space in your daily life to everything that favors your dream and helps you to strengthen your relationships. Everything that distances you, distracts you and weakens you... learn to say *no*. Why do you have the need to look good and say *yes* when in your heart you mean *no*? Only you know your dream, what inspires and motivates you, what moves you: go for it.

Be faithful to your pact, to the pact with yourself.

Look for help, space and silences. The environments in which we normally live and work are highly dysfunctional for these kinds of deep changes. Look for the help of physical spaces, people, books, groups and, above all, daily moments for this reflection.

As a minimum do a **daily review** in order to measure the level of contentment, of happiness, of enjoyment, of enthusiasm and of acceptance.

Ask yourself: what direction are you going in?

Observe what made you get angry, feel bitterness, another bad feeling or bad mood. What happened inside you for you to feel alone. Where did the wave of sadness come from? Review yourself in order to discover what you have to change, transform and/or let go of. Review yourself in order to change, not to make yourself feel guilty.

Have a **regular practice** like daily meditation, a weekly session of yoga, night-time prayer, a daily walk, etc. Maintaining times, spaces and energies to go deeper into our spiritual discovery and development is one of the tools that offers better results.

The power of writing

Early each morning you can write through creative writing. Write openly about everything that you want to, what you feel, what there is in you, what you perceive, how you want your life to be, write letting go, don't repress yourself, let the pencil, fountain pen or pen run freely over the blank page. You write this for yourself. Putting into words what you feel will help you to let go of it, to clarify it, to verbalize it. It will help you to clean what there is hidden inside your being, in your subconscious mind, in your inner store cupboards.

The power of the brake

Put a full stop. Put the brakes into action and brake. You stop for a few moments, you go back, you go inside yourself — like the tortoise —, you calm your senses and look within yourself. You control the mental traffic and you redirect your energy in the direction that you want. You go into that instance of silence and clarity emerges, the intuition speaks. In that instance you have freed yourself of the pressures.

Practice putting a full stop as many times as you can, a minute each hour is ideal.

Conscious breathing

Breathing is the metaphor of the acceptance of life; on breathing in we accept life. Breathing in is to accept and to breathe out is to contribute. It is our way of receiving the world on being born: a deep breathing in and returning of the air is our first contribution. Breathing helps us to connect to the inner silence, especially when the mind generates a lot of noise. Leading your attention to your breathing helps you to be here, centered. The transforming element in this practice is not the breathing technique nor the visualization that you might do while you are consciously breathing, it is rather the awareness that you bring to the process. Now breathe deeply, relax, give thanks and, on letting go of the air, you give yourself to the world, you hand yourself over. And in this giving of yourself is life.

Good mood and laughter

Laughter is always new, calming and quieting the mind, it unburdens, relaxes, massages the stomach and the spirit. In the moment that we laugh from the heart, we go into the Alpha state.

Use the intuition

Read the chapter 'Intuition' again in order to understand and better absorb how to open yourself to it.

Give consciously

Be generous to yourself and to others.

Give yourself permission

Give yourself permission to act in another way, to be daring, to change the center of attention.

Explore 'non-doing'

That is, go into the space of contemplation, of emptiness or of silence. Learn to do without effort. When you stop giving strength to your ego in action, when you are capable of laughing at yourself when the ego acts, and you no longer pay attention to the ego, finally it will die of hunger.

Prayer

In the space of prayer you open yourself with humility and receive the energy of the Lord.

Meditation

If we relax our body, we quieten our mind and tranquilize our heart; we will be able to connect to the impulses that come from our essence. We will discover the enormous wealth of our inner self.

15

Creative Meditation

Meditation helps you to concentrate. With concentration you can stabilize yourself in an experience. Without concentration, you only sustain it temporarily, it escapes you. With concentration, you transform the state of being under another influence and you can relax into being the owner of your own life.

For this chapter I have used the ideas of Mike George from his reflections *Clear Thinking*. The following is an excerpt from his work: You are by 'nature' a peaceful being. You are in 'essence' a silent being. You are at the very 'core' of your being completely and utterly still. You are the still point of awareness around which the world spins. So say most of the world's wisdom paths. But right now, as the 'world' tells you of its various ills and woes it's likely you feel far from being peaceful, being silent and being still. The purpose of meditation is not to make a journey, not to work hard in some effortful inner endeavor, it is simply to restore awareness of the silent and still core that is you, know the peace that is your nature and allow the love that is your purpose to emerge naturally from your heart without distortion. And in so doing the world loses its power to shake you.

To some that sounds like giving up and doing nothing! But the purpose of meditation is not to do nothing, become passive and give up all your outer responsibilities.

- It is to restore you to your true and natural inner state, so that you can draw on the power that is your silence to discern with greater clarity what you need to do.
- It is to use the power inherent in the stillness of your being to be like a rock that is smashed by the waves of the sea

and yet remains stable and unmoved.

- It is to draw on the power of your peace to cut through the clamorous noise of the world around you that is constantly demanding your attention and your energy.
- And it is to listen with your 'inner ear' to the still small voice that is the wisdom of your heart. Everyone has that voice but few can hear it amid the noise of incessant thinking and emotional turmoil. Meditation is a way of slowing and quieting the machinations of the monkey mind.

You are unlikely to do this until:

- you've had enough of that clamorous world
- your mind seems to be driving you crazy
- you're tired of your emotional exhaustion
- you have had a small taste of the peace and the power of your being
- you follow the still small voice at the core of you that invites you to sit down, be quiet and just listen.

While it sounds like there must be a right way to meditate, a 'technique' of meditation, there isn't. There are always methods and techniques to fix processes, to drive vehicles, to operate machines, to 'do' things, but there is no technique, no method to 'be'. In truth the question 'how do you meditate' is irrelevant. It is like asking 'how do you be' when you are already being and can not be because you are always being! But you are not aware of 'being', and therefore not aware of the power and the peace of your being. And that is because your attention is almost totally lost in what you are thinking, feeling and doing or on what others are doing, almost all the time. And that is why **just becoming aware of your attention, and where it goes, is the beginning of meditation**. Hence the simplest definition of meditation is the 'cultivation of self awareness' which is another way of saying being aware of you the being...being!

Ultimately there are no 'types' of meditation because as soon as you label meditation with a 'type' it appears there are different ways or methods to meditate. But there is only one way to be and it's not a 'way', it's just being. When meditation is typecast it also gives the impression that there are some ways that are superior to others, that there are better ways into being, but there aren't really. There is simply a being that is aware of being, and nothing more is needed other than being aware when attention goes away from being, gets lost in 'what' is not the self while mistaking 'it' for the self.

When that happens 'being' loses self-awareness and is trapped in ideas and images of the world, which usually begin with an idea and image of one's body. This can sound easy and obvious in theory but it is challenging to put into practice.

Almost all the habits of attention that you have learned take you away from being aware of your self and into the ideas and images of the world. And that is why you become vulnerable to any sudden and not so sudden changes to a world that is always and forever changing!

When you do sit down to meditate by all means focus your eyes on a candle or a picture, but unless you go beyond your awareness of the candle/picture it's nothing more than a short **concentration** exercise.

By all means put some relaxing music on in the background, but unless you go beyond the sound so that you no longer hear it, it's likely to be nothing more than pleasant **relaxation**.

By all means listen to a meditation commentary, but unless you, the self-aware being, actually go where the commentary is pointing, assuming it's pointing at your own being, it's not much more than **hypnosis**.

And by all means find that special place, perhaps with special people, all sitting together in a special configuration in a special posture with thumbs touching forefingers in that 'special' way, but until all that becomes completely un-special, ordinary and unnecessary then it is little more than a *comfortable trap*, and soon you, the being, will start to think that meditation is not possible, that being is not possible, unless and until you are comfortable in your trap...so to speak.

However, while all of the above can be seen as good preparations for meditation, they should not be mistaken for meditation itself.

In meditation you are returning to the place where you always are without going anywhere or doing anything. In time, and with practice, this will eventually require no time and no practice, simply because 'pure being' is beyond time and needs to do nothing in order to act appropriately and effectively! But in between here and there, between now and then, a combination of ideas (signposts) and a kind of inner effort is required. Not least the 'seeing' of what stops you being fully present where you are, what stops you from being aware of being the being that you are.

Some initial guidance and signposts are as follows.

Learning to read

Wouldn't be wonderful if we could sit in meditation and just be? And when we are just being we would be at peace with ourselves and with the world. And sometimes, when you meditate, you will know this state, you will touch and taste this state, a state where you may even lose awareness of time and place. But of course it's momentary and in its place comes distraction in many forms, and that's when attention is attracted and starts wandering. And this is where meditation is like reading.

When you look at the words on a page, when you look at those little black 'letter' symbols on a white background, they have no meaning, they make no sense, as long as they remain on the page. It's only when you bring them into your consciousness and the single symbols (letters) form collective symbols (words and sentences) that you begin to ascribe meaning. You are the ascriber, and meaning is your ascription. Which of course is why five different people can attribute different meanings to the same collection of word symbols.

In almost exactly the same way symbols will appear within your consciousness when you meditate and you can learn to ascribe meaning to those symbols. As you do you will come to see and understand why you find it hard to just be your self. These symbols are what we call thoughts, emotions, perceptions and beliefs. They all arise within you and as they do you will have the opportunity to 'see' and 'know' what they mean.

As you learn to 'read' these inner signs you will begin to understand what is distracting you from truly being the being that you are. And then you will see how YOU get trapped in those thoughts/emotions etc, and as you get trapped in them you give them more power. Meditation happens when you don't 'go in' but 'pull out' of what arises within consciousness. And the more you pull out the weaker they become until eventually they don't arise.

Like reading a book and, in many ways, like watching a movie, all you have to do is sit quietly and watch what arises within your consciousness. If you can do that without resisting or empowering whatever arises you will start to see why you have created and are creating those mental and emotional distractions in the first place. You will start to see what their presence 'means'. You will see exactly why they are distracting the peace of your being, you will see how they cloud and skew your ability to make good decisions, and you will see how they can make you vulnerable to the changing world around you.

A very small sample of what can you expect to see arise within your consciousness and what they mean are as follows.

You will see thoughts arising that are agitative. Controlling, judgmental and critical thoughts mean you are still carrying and holding onto a belief that it's your job to fix others and the world which, when seen in the light of meditation, is clearly nonsense.

You may feel the emotions of shame and guilt arising frequently, which means you are still holding onto a belief that you are bad person who does bad things. This also becomes nonsense as soon as you glimpse the heart of your heart, which you will realize is a source of love and joy in the world and that they can never be diminished, only suppressed.

You will see and feel the habitual arising of emotions such as fear and sadness, and if you sit quietly with such emotions you will be able to trace their origins back to your attachment to a belief that you can possess 'things' and 'people'. This will also become nonsensical as you realize you cannot possess anything or anyone. You cannot even possess your body, only occupy it.

And gradually what were emotional tsunamis, sucking up your energy, which is YOU, subside to occasional ripples across the surface of your consciousness. Until they are no more.

So as you watch what arises you will see much non-sense. And you will notice how it keeps you trapped in a jungle of thoughts and emotions that constitute misery to some degree or other. You will also begin to notice that while certain people and situations seem to 'trigger' your emotional disturbances they don't 'cause' them. And is you 'notice' this so the habit of blaming will atrophy – always a good measure of how your meditation is deepening your awareness of you, and a good measure that means your meditation is working.

When you practice meditation you are really practicing being aware of what is getting your attention and being attentive to what is filling your awareness. And as you do you will see all that is not you, but seems to be you. In other words you are not the thoughts, emotions, beliefs, perceptions, attitudes that arise within you. They arise, they are there, they are your creation, but they are not you.

They are like extreme weather patterns flitting across the surface of the world. They always pass. And when stormy weather passes only peace and tranquility remain, only beauty and harmony remain. And the natural world just gets on with what it has to do within that harmony. And so it is within consciousness, within your self.

The storms of negative thoughts can rage, the winds of emotion can sweep through your consciousness in a second. They appear and then they disappear, and when the self sees the ultimate powerlessness of such patterns the self ceases to empower them, allowing them die away, leaving peace and tranquility, beauty and harmony to emerge. Until one day, they also remain. That'll be today!

16

The Inner Kingdom

In the next chapters we will see how, from the inner kingdom of each one of us, we can create a new world. First, the inner kingdom has to renew itself, then we go from individual power to the power of the group in order to, finally, create a collective, a community that vibrates on the vibration of the new world. That way the new earth will emerge.

In this chapter the subheadings are:

- *New thoughts*
- *New attitudes*
- *New values*

The Old and New Testament speak to us of the collapse of the existing world order and the emergence of a new heaven and a new earth.

They make references to the inner kingdom of the consciousness and its external manifestation in form, as a reflection of the inner: a new earth.

Isaiah says (65:17):

... For past problems will be forgotten;

I will no longer think about them. For look, I am ready to create new heavens and a new earth! The former ones will not be remembered; no one will think about them anymore. But be happy and rejoice forevermore over what I am about to create! (...) A wolf and a lamb will graze together; a lion, like an ox, will eat straw. They will no longer injure or destroy on my entire royal mountain," says the LORD.

Isaiah 60:21:

All of your people will be godly; they will possess the land permanently. I will plant them like a shoot; they will be the product of my labor.

Revelation 21:1:

Then I saw a new heaven and a new earth, (...) and death will not exist any more – or mourning, or crying, or pain, for the former things have ceased to exist." (...) And the one seated on the throne said: "Look! I am making all things new!" Then he said to me, "Write it down, because these words are reliable and true."

What has to happen in the inner kingdom so that the creation of a new world is generated? Do we have such power as to create a new earth, a new civilization? We definitely do. In this chapter I will deal with the creativity that is necessary to regain your mastery over the inner kingdom and the impact that this creates in the world.

We have such a potential of love in the heart of our being that we could heal the planet. If our hearts were to unite in the essential of being, we would achieve a miraculous transformation. First we should begin by loving ourselves. Creating a centered, silent and loving attitude, we shall create a secure atmosphere and we will generate a healing and transforming space.

The newness in the world should begin with the individual. Through a change in his or her consciousness that leads to a generation of new attitudes, new thoughts, new values and new feelings.

New thoughts

It does not take any more effort to create a positive thought than a negative one. However, there are few people who build positive thoughts that lead us to attitudes and behavior that help us. We think through past associations, and not through the present moment.

We can create new thoughts on going beyond our inner chatter of automatic, superfluous and mechanical thoughts. It is to leave behind chemical, cerebral and mental addiction. Each thought generates a neuronal response in the brain, producing chemical substances to which the brain and the body become addicted. The routine thoughts maintain the chemical substances in the brain at its usual levels, and, therefore, they do not generate change or newness.

We can create innovative thoughts out of an awakened and aware consciousness, attentive and observing, curious and open.

New attitudes

- An attitude of genuinely embracing life and people: disinterestedly, altruistic and generous. With acceptance. An inclusive attitude.
- An attitude of courage to face things and let go. To transform. To be, without masks.
- An attitude of gratitude, not of obligation. Giving thanks for the fact of existing. The sun comes out each day. Do you give thanks for it? Do you enjoy it?
- An attitude of innocence, like that of a child on making a discovery.
- Being like a child, with curiosity to explore, know, adventure, learn, and like a wise person: with maturity, mastery and inner serenity.
- An attitude of compassion instead of anger. Let us understand that, with anger, we use the same energy that created the injustice, our love dries up, provoking more violence and we do not change the injustice. Compassion requires wisdom, depth, forgiveness, detachment, discernment, patience. Compassion is understanding and love.

To awaken and express these attitudes we need attention. If not, it is easy to go back to the comfort of our habitual attitudes and fall into complaining, anger, blaming or senseless criticizing.

It is about leaving behind the habits of being depressed, furious, in bad moods, pressurized, bitter, full of hate and moving on to feel happy, joyful, satisfied and encouraged. It is a question of making one's mind up to it.

New values

To transform yourself is to break with the custom of being who you are accustomed to being and connecting to the deepest and most essential of yourself. To do so, you should free yourself from a hyperactive, stressful and overly busy life that flattens your spirit and that has taken over you. Incorporate values such as silence, quietness, observation and patience. We have to generate the space that is necessary to enter into a state of being in which the gears of change can get going.

The new values connect us to the authentic and the true. Leaving behind mirages and defense mechanisms. Leaving behind the culture of pretending and the materialist values that break the harmony with nature, with others and with ourselves.

Values that lead us to different and new forms of learning. Deeper forms of perceiving, of seeing beyond the apparent.

17

From the Individual to the Collective

The people who have awoken to this new form of essential being, without masks, with humility and personal power, without submission, with these new thoughts, feelings, attitudes and values, will gather together in a harmonious way. In a natural way, they will join together to create a new culture, a new civilization.

There will be complementarity among them, not competition or jealousy. Neither victims nor aggressors; neither oppressed nor oppressors.

An equality of feeling will be experienced: a feeling of love, generosity and unity.

There will be an equality of objective: a better world for *all*.

An equality of vision will be felt: a world in harmony, a just world.

This will arrive because each one will have done their real and transforming research, in the laboratory of their life. With practice and experience, we will be on the same vibration. We will live out a deep faith in non-violence as a lifestyle. We will share the same objectives and the same values. We will follow a similar lifestyle, based on respect towards all live beings. A simple and austere lifestyle. The group acts as *one* out of the deep acceptance of the principle of respect.

We will understand each other without having to explain things a hundred times. We will experience a practical telepathy: be able to communicate our thoughts and understand each other. Real telepathy that is collective. Our antennae, our conscious-nesses and minds will be clean of unnecessary thoughts and disturbing noises.

We will be a group of people working together, with a

collective consciousness, to create a new world. Consciousness here on the earth, centered in time and space.

As far as the group that lives together and acts thus is concerned, perhaps there will be mention of the name of the group, as one mentions the hand, but the names of the people, the names of the fingers and thumb, will not be singled out. Each finger of the hand is different; nevertheless, they are joined and they work together. They arise out of the same essence and work for a same task. They accompany each other. There is no desire to stand out or to wear medals. A group or community that has reached this level of collective consciousness will have respect for the specialties of each one: each one is important for the collective work.

For example, a group like that reminds us of the angels. Some names in particular are remembered, but it is said that there are thousands of angels, and they are spoken of in general; of their presence, task and shared mission.

18

The New Earth

To create a new world, a new earth, we need to have a vision of how we want it to be. That way we can focus our energy and effort on creating and living it.

Paradise was a period before we learned to live in our minds. A period in which we did not have confusions about being, about who I am. A period in which our humanity and our character were transparent, nobody had anything to hide or cover up. A period in which an embrace was much more than a physical gesture of greeting each other and human warmth. When a heart met with another in a subtle dance that said not only, "I love you," but, "I am love for you."

In nature and in life everything works in cycles. Paradise was and will be again. I transmit here some ideas to envision the new world. I use the verb in the present form. Imagine while you read it that you are living it now.

On this new earth we feel secure, we are safe: there is no violence at all.

You feel strong, sure of yourself. There is no provocation or criticism (they are forms of aggression). Respect is natural, it is in the air, in the atmosphere. The security that you feel is natural, you don't even think about it, and therefore fear does not exist even in your thinking.

You live in authenticity, without masks. You have nothing to hide.

We live the gentleness, the tenderness, the sensitivity and the sweetness in our being. There is neither rigidity nor hardness.

You do not need to analyze: there is natural intuition. What is the origin of our intuition? It is the legacy of this time in which we live in harmony and we do not create either solid or subtle barriers inside us, not among ourselves and not with the world.

There is health and prosperity. The body is not mistreated with bad feelings, bad thoughts, bad postures, damaging habits or unhealthy food. Because there is no greed and, therefore, the wealth belongs to everyone and is distributed from the awareness of abundance, not from the narrow mentality of shortage. Nobody is lacking the essential.

On the new earth no one has emotional, mental or physical deficiencies. Everyone feels full, be it the gardener, the tailor or the king.

One never arrives late, one never runs to get anywhere. One arrives at the right time. All is well in this moment.

Relationships complement each other and do not compete among themselves. Relationships are not possessive. Each one is free. The inner freedom of each one eliminates any tendency of dependence. There is no dependence that arises out of selfish need.

You are free, complete and whole: you neither depend nor need. There is no addiction.

In communication you only say what you mean; what each person wants to say is transmitted and expressed without room for misunderstandings. The capacity for listening is global: we listen to the soul, the look, the thought, the feeling, the intention, the gesture, the word. Not everything is said, not because we are hiding anything, but because we also communicate in a non-verbal form: our vibration communicates.

There is companionship, friendship and trust. Relationships are lasting, deep and permanent. We do not separate; rather we complement each other basing ourselves on respect, difference and creative shared living.

Relationships are inclusive. For example, there is not the exclusivity of 'my children'. We will feel the children of the neighbors as our own.

There is harmony in the soul, with the body, nature and between people.

Let's begin to live this now. Let us get back our power of will in order to concentrate on what deserves it, on the essential and on what will provide us with energy and strength to take the necessary extraordinary leap to create this new earth.

To end this section on the Golden Age, I reproduce the texts on Paradise written by Barbara Ramsay, for the Spiritual Love and Wisdom Art Gallery, Agra, 2003. The religious writings and the legacy of ancient civilizations speak to us of the existence of an Earthly Paradise. Barbara and I made a study of all those texts and writings for the creation of two Galleries of Spiritual Art in India, one at Mount Abu and the other in Agra. These texts sum up the essence of this vision of Paradise found in different sources.

In the Golden Age
There was love of many things in that time, but the first love was the one that lived peacefully behind each one's eyes. The truth of that love became like a mirror and each one saw their reflection in the eyes of the others, shining with beauty and grace. And we lived gently with each other.

In the Perfect Age
In this time people filled with honour and fairness all the sweet corners of their minds. And the truth of our world was equality – not imposed by law or enforced by circumstance, but springing from an inherent knowledge of the natural laws of the universe.

In Paradise
With every day that passed, with every movement of the sun, the time was always 'now'. And 'now' held a lifetime of possibilities. For in that almost forgotten age, a human being's days

were long and filled with laughter. Beauty was the colour of the world and joy was as natural as breathing.

In Satyuga (The Era of Truth)
Your thoughts were easy and crystal and rang gently like a speaking breeze. You lived as kings then and nature did your bidding, for your life had a harmony with all things. Love and respect for each other was the pattern of the days and so every soul blossomed into all the best things they could possibly be.

In Heaven on Earth
Time treated you gently. The days of your lives were long and the air sang with the hidden music of your tranquil joy.

This was a time of true civilization. Not a civilization of great cities and the structures of power. In this time, science worked naturally with humanity and nature and made life for every soul a thing of harmony and ease.

This time was ours and as the cycle of time turns, carrying every living being with it, we will return to that heaven where our hearts were happiest.

Jesus said to his disciples:

The kingdom of God is not coming with signs to be observed, nor will they say, 'Look, here it is!' or 'There!' For indeed, the kingdom of God is in your midst (Luke 17:20-21).

That is, it will not be in a future, but is rather now. Only when it is now in you, will it begin to be so around you, until we reach the critical number of awakened consciousnesses that will generate global change and the new earth will be created.

Bibliographical References

It is inspiring to see how the world balance is changing. It seems that there is a return to living less in the rational process and more in the intuitive consciousness. The explosion of cognitive therapies, personal coaching, meditation, the growing interest in emotional and spiritual intelligence, are signs that, for many, the materialist rational programming has run its course.

There are more and more authors who publish books that connect us to the truth that we are the creators of our personal and collective reality, and that it is in our hands to change and create the world that we want to create and in which we want to live.

In this book I have quoted various authors:

Eckhart Tolle, in his book *A New Earth*, clearly explains to us the difference between the ego and the consciousness of the soul. He inspires us to build a new earth. Penguin Group, 2006.

Karol K. Truman, *Feelings Buried Alive Never Die...*, Olympus Publishing, EEUU, 2007.

Eric Rolf, *Soul Medicine*.

Louise L. Hay, *You Can Heal Your Life*, Hay House, EEUU, 2004.

Joe Dispenza, *Evolve Your Brain: The Science of Changing Your Mind*.

Karol K. Truman, Eric Rolf, Louise L. Hay and Joe Dispenza clarify for us the influence of our thoughts and feelings on our body, our health and our illness.

The Cloud of Unknowing, by an English monk of the fourteenth century.

Swami Amar Jyoti, *Retreat into Eternity, An Upanishad Book of Aphorisms*, published by Truth Consciousness, USA, 1981.

Hafiz, *The Gift*, Penguin, New York, 1999.

The Cloud of Unknowing, Retreat into Eternity and *The Gift* are three books that allow us to return to the essence of the spiritual message. One is from the Christian tradition, another Hindu and another Muslim, but, in their essence, they take us to the spirituality that transcends the religions and unites the souls.

Anthony Strano, spiritual teacher and without whom this book would not be as what it is, has published various books. One that is still unpublished, *Exploring the Four Movements*, is the one I quote in the pages of this book. It is the essence of what life itself is and can be.

Concerning the Spiritual in Art, by Wassily Kandinsky, seems to me to be of exquisite wealth. How good it is that artists open themselves to spirituality, and reflect, work and create from that dimension.

Mike George regularly writes some reflections that he sends to hundreds of people, with the title *Clear Thinking*. I have used two of them:

- On intuition: *Clear Thinking* Nº 84, October 2007.
- On meditation: *Clear Thinking* Nº 44, 30th November 2008.

For more information, see www.relax7.com

Experiments in Silence is a journal published by the Brahma Kumaris World Spiritual University and the Fetzer Institute of the USA. It was published in 2003 as the result of the dialogue series, *Call of the time*. From it I have taken quotes from Dadi Janki and inspiration from Judy Rodgers and Gayatri Naraine for the theme of the *Mansa Seva*. For more information, see www.callofthetime.com

I have mentioned my already published books:

Miriam Subirana Vilanova

Who Rules in Your Life? Co-author: Ramón Ribalta Secanell (First published in Spanish in 2003). O Books, UK 2008.

Dare to Live. Reflections on Fear, Courage and Wholeness (First published in Spanish in 2007). O Books, UK 2008.

Live in Freedom. Reflections on Limits, Dreams and the Essential (First published in Spanish in 2008). O Books, UK 2009.

For the references to the Greek goddesses I have used a book of Greek mythology:

Sofia Souli, *Greek Mythology, the Creation of the Gods, the Gods, the Heroes, the Trojan War, the Odyssey.* Toubis Editions, Attiki, Greece 1995.

The Bible used in the English translation is the Net Bible (www.net.bible.org).

BOOKS

O is a symbol of the world, of oneness and unity. In different cultures it also means the "eye," symbolizing knowledge and insight. We aim to publish books that are accessible, constructive and that challenge accepted opinion, both that of academia and the "moral majority."

Our books are available in all good English language bookstores worldwide. If you don't see the book on the shelves ask the bookstore to order it for you, quoting the ISBN number and title. Alternatively you can order online (all major online retail sites carry our titles) or contact the distributor in the relevant country, listed on the copyright page.

See our website **www.o-books.net** for a full list of over 500 titles, growing by 100 a year.

And tune in to myspiritradio.com for our book review radio show, hosted by June-Elleni Laine, where you can listen to the authors discussing their books.